# The Nature of Early Greek Lyric: Three Preliminary Studies

Three important literary questions in early Greek lyric are addressed in this study. First, Fowler attempts to determine the extent that Homer and epic poetry generally influenced the lyric poets, with respect to both the style of compositions and their content. Identifying the certain examples of influence – which are far fewer than often thought – he analyses the technique of imitation, tracing a development from simpler to more complex as the archaic period proceeds. Throughout this and the following chapter, he often finds occasion to take issue with the famous and influential view of the early Greek mind championed by Bruno Snell and Hermann Fränkel.

In the second chapter Fowler studies the organization of individual poems, identifying compositional principles that may be used to solve literary and textual problems. Some of these principles, like ring-composition, are old familiars; others are not. All are found to be more pervasive than is often realized, and reflect an attitude to composition rather different from the disorderly and associative techniques traditionally ascribed to the lyric poets.

The last chapter explores the nature of genres in the archaic period, starting from the vexed question of the definition of elegy. In all the genres associated with particular occasions, the author finds that the poets' professional skills and self-consciousness became more important than the purely occasional aspects of their compositions. Observations of interest are made on, among others, citharodic songs, epigrams and epinician odes; and elegy in the end turns out, paradoxically, not to be a true genre at all.

ROBERT L. FOWLER is Associate Professor of Classical Studies, University of Waterloo.

PHOENIX

Journal of the Classical Association of Canada
Revue de la Société canadienne des études classiques
Supplementary Volume XXI
Tome supplémentaire XXI

R.L. FOWLER

# The Nature of
# Early Greek Lyric:
# Three Preliminary Studies

UNIVERSITY OF TORONTO PRESS
Toronto  Buffalo  London

©University of Toronto Press 1987
Toronto Buffalo London
Printed in Canada
ISBN 0-8020-5714-4

Printed on acid-free paper

**Canadian Cataloguing in Publication Data**

Fowler, R.L. (Robert Louis), 1954–
The nature of early Greek lyric

(Phoenix Supplementary volume ISSN 0079-1784; 21)
Includes bibliographical references and index.
ISBN 0-8020-5714-4

1. Greek poetry – History and criticism. I. Title.
II. Series: Phoenix. Supplementary volume (Toronto, Ont.); 21

PA3110.F69 1987     884'.01     C87-093093-1

This book has been published with
the help of a grant from
the Canadian Federation for the Humanities,
using funds provided by the Social Sciences and
Humanities Research Council of Canada.

# CONTENTS

DIS MANIBUS SACRUM
L.H. FOWLER, D.D.
PATRIS PIENTISSIMI

†21 VI 1981

... ἐμνήσθην ὁσσάκις ἀμφότεροι
ἥλιον ἐν λέσχηι κατεδύσαμεν ...

# PREFACE

The magnificent efforts of philologists in recent years have ensured that the textual basis for the study of Greek lyric is fairly secure, so it seems time to reassess some old questions of a general nature, and perhaps to ask a few new ones. I have selected three: the influence of Homer on early lyric poetry; structural devices and narrative technique; and the definition of 'elegy' in comparison with other genres. This is therefore a work of the *Quaestiones selectae* variety, only the various *quaestiones* are not entirely distinct and self-contained. While there is no obvious external unity, there are many small links between the chapters, of which I become more aware the longer I live with the work. I suppose what I am trying to describe, at least in part, is the nature of early Greek lyric, whence the title; but I do not wish to claim too much by it. Another overriding concern may be described as historical: to understand how this fascinating period of Greek literature bridged the gap between Homer and the fifth century.

Pindar, Bacchylides, and other fifth-century lyricists are largely excluded from this study; for each of the topics here treated, especially narrative technique and genre, they might require a separate book. That is not only a function of the amount of surviving poetry. It will be clear from what is said in the book that the lyric poets of the late archaic period were beginning to write a type of lyric that differed in kind, in nature, from that of their predecessors. Not that there was a conscious or sharp break; rather it is a matter of a tradition being summed up and transcended. What is said here may be regarded as a preface to a book that could be written on the later lyric poets.

I feel obliged to warn readers that a good deal of Chapters 1 and 2 has been devoted to a thorough critique of views best associated with Hermann Fränkel and Bruno Snell. Some will feel this is a dead horse and others will regret the amount of time spent in negative criticism. The horse, however, is very much alive. In books and articles recently written one still reads of the 'lyric age,' or the limitations of the paratactic style, or subtle modifications of Homeric models. The works of these brilliant scholars have had a pervasive influence and indeed may have become part of our subconscious attitude; *The Discovery of the Mind* and *Early Greek Poetry and Philosophy* are works to be found on countless undergraduate reading lists. Moreover, a study of the methodological strengths and limitations of these works, which made their first appearance some sixty years ago, becomes in itself a chapter in the history of twentieth-century classical scholarship; one gains a clear sense of the opposite extreme to which many critics now tend of emphasizing the generic and the traditional to the total exclusion of the individual. This approach too has its problems.

A second warning, or apology, has to do with the analyses offered in Chapter 2. In order to prove the thesis of the chapter adequately it is necessary to look at a great number of poems. But to treat them all as they deserve to be treated would create a book of great length and add more notes where there are probably too many to begin with. As a compromise I have first discussed the Cologne fragment of Alcaeus in detail as a test case. Passages of special relevance are similarly treated; but often I have had simply to give my own view or endorse someone else's with a minimum of argument. References to more complete discussions and critical controversy are duly given in the notes for those who might otherwise be misled.

The book originated as an Oxford DPhil thesis (1980), but it has been completely rewritten. The necessary leisure was afforded by a fellowship at the Calgary Institute for the Humanities in the University of Calgary. The cost of preparing the manuscript for publication was met in part by a research grant from the University of Waterloo.

At various stages in the work's gestation I have profited from the kind criticisms of others, whose names I am eager to record. Professors Martin West and L.E. Rossi provided valuable comments on drafts of Chapter 3. Professor Doktor Rudolf Kassel read through the whole in an earlier form, putting his judgment and learning completely at my disposal, and taking time out from a busy schedule to acquaint a beginner with the great tradition of scholarship behind him. The thesis in its final state was much improved by the suggestions of Dr G.O. Hutchinson of Exeter College, Oxford, Professors Martin Cropp and John Yardley of Calgary, and especially of my examiners, Sir Kenneth Dover and Mr D.A. Russell. The draft of the book was then closely scrutinized by the editor of the *Phoenix* Supplementary Volumes, Professor M.B. Wallace, and two anonymous readers, and the final manuscript was edited by Mr Fred Unwalla for the University of

Toronto Press. Professor Emmet Robbins of St Michael's College, Toronto, added his keen observations. Professor Christopher Brown and Mr Blake Johnson were then kind enough to assist in the task of reading the proofs, the former adding important criticism.

I owe a special debt to the late Professor Leonard Woodbury, who first awakened my interest in this field, and taught me its problems.

Most of all I am indebted to Hugh Lloyd-Jones. It was a windfall for a young man at my stage of studies to have him as a teacher; those who have been his pupils know what it means.

γραμματικὸς κριτικός θ' ὅδ' ἀνήρ· χάριτας δὲ φίλοισιν
ἢν ἐθέλεις εἰπεῖν, ἄλλοσε μήποθ' ὅρα.

Waterloo, Ontario
19 V 1984

# ABBREVIATIONS

Abbreviations follow those in the second edition of the *Oxford Classical Dictionary*; if an author or journal is not listed in that publication, the abbreviation follows LSJ for the former, *L'Année philologique* for the latter. Exceptions will readily explain themselves.
Please note the following:

| | |
|---|---|
| *Archiloque* | *Archiloque Entretiens Hardt* 10 (Geneva 1963) |
| Burnett, *Three Archaic Poets* | Anne Pippin Burnett, *Three Archaic Poets: Archilochus, Alcaeus, Sappho* (Cambridge, Mass. 1983) |
| Fränkel, *Dichtung und Philosophie* | H. Fränkel, *Dichtung und Philosophie des frühen Griechentums* (München ³1968) |
| – *Wege und Formen* | id, *Wege und Formen frühgriechischen Denkens* (München ³1968) |
| Hansen | P.A. Hansen, ed *Carmina Epigraphica Graeca Saeculorum VIII–V a. Chr. n.* (Berlin and New York 1983) |
| LSJ | Liddell and Scott, ed *A Greek-English Lexicon* rev. H. Stuart Jones (⁹1940) *With a Supplement* (1968) |
| Page, *Sappho and Alcaeus* | D.L. Page, *Sappho and Alcaeus* (Oxford 1955) |

| | |
|---|---|
| PLF | *Poetarum Lesbiorum Fragmenta,* ed E. Lobel and D.L. Page (Oxford 1955) |
| PMG | *Poetae Melici Graeci,* ed D.L. Page (Oxford 1962). Fragments are cited according to the continuous numeration. |
| RE | A. Pauly, G. Wissowa, *et al, Realencyclopädie der klass- ischen Altertumswissenschaft* (1893– ). |
| SLG | *Supplementum Lyricis Graecis,* ed D.L. Page (Oxford 1974). Fragments are cited in the form 's478.' |
| V(oigt) | E.-M. Voigt, ed *Sappho et Alcaeus* (Amsterdam 1971) |
| Vors. | *Die Fragmente der Vorsokratiker,* ed H. Diels, 6. Aufl. v. W. Kranz (1951–2) |
| West, *Iambi et Elegi* | M.L. West, ed *Iambi et Elegi Graeci* 2 vols (Oxford 1971–2) |
| – *Studies* | id, *Studies in Greek Elegy and Iambus* (Berlin 1974) |
| Wilamowitz, *Sappho und Simonides* | U. von Wilamowitz-Moellendorff, *Sappho und Simonides* (Berlin 1913) |

The lyric poets are cited from the editions in this list (Sappho and Alcaeus from Voigt, with equivalent numbers from PLF given when desirable – suffix 'LP'); Pindar and Bacchylides from the Teubner editions of B. Snell and H. Maehler; and the fragments of Hesiod from the edition of R. Merkelbach and M.L. West ('M-W').

Es läßt sich eben auch die Stilentwickelung eines Volkes nicht a priori feststellen, für die Griechen aber ist es immer noch nötig, solche Constructionen a priori zu beseitigen, was dann zunächst nur zu oft mit dem Eingeständnis unseres Nichtwissens zusammengeht.

Ulrich von Wilamowitz-Moellendorff,
*Sappho und Simonides* 128.

The Nature of Early Greek Lyric

# 1

# Homer and the Lyric Poets

The influence of the epic on Greek lyric poetry[1] is obvious and extensive. One of the first steps therefore in any study of lyric as a type of literature might be to consider its relations to Homer. An innocent might begin by tracing the connections between, say, Archilochus and Homer, as one would between any other two authors: find the parallels, determine which ones indicate direct dependence, describe how the poet has altered his models. Unfortunately, things are not so simple.

We find that Archilochus seems to imitate some passages from Homer, and uses a fair number of phrases taken from the epic. Well and good; but how are we to evaluate the significance of this situation? Are Archilochus' epic-like phrases being used as Homer uses his formulae? Some scholars have thought so. Does that mean that Archilochus is an oral poet? What is a formula, anyway? How does one oral poet imitate another? Does Archilochus imitate Homer's text in a form more or less like the text we know now? If he has introduced modifications in the process of borrowing, is his reason for doing so purely literary, or is it some cultural reason, some changed social value that no longer permits Homer's words to be used in their original form? Are we to say, with many scholars, that the complex relation of lyric and epic poetry is not so much a literary phenomenon as the product of a cultural revolution, the succession of the so-called Epic Age by the Lyric Age?

All of these are legitimate questions, which the student encounters early in his or her study. What is happening here is that the poetry of archaic Greece, as the chief evidence for the period's cultural and intellectual history, is being made to do extra duty. The poetry looms much larger in this period than in later ones, for which we have extensive prose writings and a greater number of monuments. There are two very great dangers, however: first, in assuming that the poetry by itself can offer a completely faithful account of contemporary society in all its complexity; and second, in indulging the temptation to fill in the many gaps in the record of the poetry, which is of course preserved in a very fragmentary state.

Existing attempts to reconstruct the cultural history of early Greece have not avoided these dangers. The attempt, however, must be made, since one's answer to any one of the questions listed above will affect one's understanding of many poems. It is unfortunate that all of them are extremely controversial questions, which I will not be able to treat with justice. Still, it is necessary to state my views, if only with a minimum of argument. Perhaps more important is the need to say why existing views are wrong, not for any love of destructive criticism, but because of the great influence they continue to exert.

We may first consider the ambitious theory of what may be called the 'Fränkel-Snell school.' Translations of works by these two great scholars and their followers have long been standard reading for undergraduates.[2] Those who might be skeptical of some of their views are probably affected at least subconsciously by others. Despite the relatively long reign of their orthodoxy, no exhaustive critique of their theory has been published, although several scholars have challenged particular aspects.[3] Generations of students and teachers have regarded it as axiomatic that human beings 'discovered the mind' during Archilochus' lifetime.

The theory of these writers runs as follows. Since the *Iliad*, *Odyssey*, Hesiod, and Archilochus form a chronological series, and since poets in Greece are the repositories of that culture's values in their ideal and quintessential form, the comparison of their works is the surest way to reconstruct the period's *Geistesgeschichte*.[4] A large part of their method (especially Snell's and Treu's) is lexicographical; the history of a concept is traced through the history of the word denoting it. The end result of their work is to describe how the 'Epic Age' gave way to the 'Lyric Age.' The age of heroism, aristocracy, and the equation of external appearance with reality, gave way to the world of the individual, the πόλις, and the discovery of inner life and emotions.

Such is their theory, in very crude outline; most readers will be able to add the details. There are serious difficulties.

1  As several scholars have pointed out, the lexicographical method is inadequate. It is simplistic and works only when evidence is limited. In the fifth century, when literary evidence is not only richer but supplemented by other sorts, exclusively lexicographical studies cannot give an accurate picture of the period's intellectual history. Our understanding of the contexts in which individual words occur is greatly enhanced, because we are

aware of a far larger number of relevant considerations. It needs no argument that an understanding of context profoundly influences our evaluation of a word's meaning. The success of the method in the study of the earlier period is illusory.

The lexicographical method also assumes that a concept cannot be present without the word which denotes it. One example will show the oddities which result from this error. Snell believes that Homer has a concept of 'character' radically different from ours, and points out that he has no word for 'will.' The heroes are incapable of making a decision on their own, he argues; instead, a god must implant the correct idea in their heads. Similarly, Homer conceives of emotions as being given to the individual by an external force. Now, a sensitive reader of the *Iliad* reacts with astonishment to this opinion; he or she knows instinctively that the text holds a great poet's portrayal of character. Jasper Griffin's recent and convincing study of Homeric characterization will confirm that appraisal.[5] The pursuit of a rigid, apparently scientific method may lead to a distorted interpretation of the poetry.

The theory also ignores the nature of epic style, and, more seriously, misapprehends the character of the Homeric gods. To take the former first: when Homer says, 'The goddess breathed strength into Diomedes,' he does not mean that the warrior is to be regarded as a lump of clay which springs to life only when invigorated by some external agent. To an extent, it is manner of speaking. One can conceive of an emotion as coming from outside – in fact we still speak this way quite often – without being ignorant that it is one's own emotion, within the body of an individual agent. When we say 'He was inspired,' it is largely a metaphorical way of speaking; we only speak as if there were an outside force.[6] For Homer such expressions cannot be mere metaphors, because the goddess who breathes strength is real; but the regularity with which he speaks in this way is a matter of epic stylization. It is an unrealistic, grand manner. Many of Homer's mannerisms are part of the tradition he inherits; they are fixed expressions in formulaic systems. Many accidental oddities are bound to appear in lexicographical statistics. But the nature of the genre is more important. Homer also has highly stylized ways of describing battles; but he must have known that in real life spears frequently do hit the general.

On the one hand, then, we must not ignore the implications of epic style. On the other hand, we must nevertheless recognize that the goddess who breathes strength is quite real. The Greeks had a power of imagination which we have lost. (I say 'imagination' for want of a better word.) Behind any aspect of human life, behind any great achievement or failure, behind any phenomenon of nature, they saw a personality whose existence you could not deny any more than you could deny the existence of the weather. Humanity and divinity were inseparably linked; for the Christian this view might belittle the divine, but for the pagan humanity is elevated. When a man won at the Olympic games, a god was behind him; the god must be credited, or the man will be presumptuous; but it is equally true that the god would not have helped him if his name were Thersites. This Olympic victory can be described in several ways: the man won; the man won with the god's help; the god arranged that the man should win. All are different ways of describing the same thing. Divine and human work on parallel planes to affect the course of events: 'double determination.'[7]

Perhaps the best known example is the Athena-Achilles episode in the first book of the *Iliad*. According to Snell, this scene shows very clearly that Homeric man is incapable of making a decision. But Athena's appearance here takes nothing away from Achilles' ability to think for himself.[8] Homer could easily have described the scene differently, emphasizing the human motivation involved, as he does in numerous other scenes. Here he sees the divine aspect more clearly; small wonder, at this juncture in the plot. The dramatic effect is also important. The vivid, concrete image which arrests and focuses the attention is typical of Greek poetry. Homer's image of Athena tugging at Achilles' hair is a brilliant example. For some scholars, her gesture emphasizes Achilles' lack of independence; however, there is no real connection with psychology at all. Similarly, when Homer shows Zeus raising the scales, he intends it to be a grand, dramatic gesture. That is the whole point. There is no comment that Zeus does not know what Fate is; still less does the scene show that Zeus, like men, is unable to make a decision on his own.[9] We need only ask ourselves: could Hephaestus lift those scales?

If we wish to find a decision-making process described solely in human terms, Hector's monologue (*Il.* 22.99–130) will do. But this is unusual, because in epic the gods must be everywhere. In the *Iliad*, there are gods fighting on either side; Zeus dispenses evil and good alike; the gods are capricious, and accountable to no one. All this is appropriate to the tragic conception of life in the poem. In the *Odyssey*, the gods again play an important role in the plot; but they are now united toward the accomplishment of good, except for Poseidon, who is absent from the assembly in Book 1, and is a symbol of evil at work. The different situation is appropriate to the generic requirements of that poem, where the 'heroes versus villains' atmosphere of the folk tale is prominent.

2 Some indication has already been given of a second difficulty: the Fränkel-Snell theory fails to consider, or consider correctly, the important effects of a poem's genre. It finds for example that Archilochus reacts against epic values; but his sentiments in a poem like fr 114 (οὐ φιλέω μέγαν

στρατηγόν) may have a much simpler significance: there really was such a general, who was the butt of iambic lampoonery. Or, in poems like fr 191 (τοῖος γὰρ φιλότητος ἔρως) and fr 193 (δύστηνος ἔγκειμαι πόθωι), we learn from Snell that love now has a 'new' inner aspect; we hear about lyric ἀμηχανία. But the pains and hopes of the individual naturally come to the foreground in lyric poetry, because that is its purpose; in epic, although 'lyric' sentiments can, significantly, occur, they are of secondary importance.

3 These thoughts lead to another difficulty: although poetry is central to Greek culture, an individual poet cannot be assumed to reflect the views of all his contemporaries. We have too little evidence from the early archaic period to evaluate the relation of the poetry to the society; the temptation to make too much of what we do have should be resisted. Because Archilochus is assumed by these scholars to be representative of his age, they conclude that the 'Lyric Age' succeeded the 'Epic Age' typified by Homer. Such a conclusion reflects a simplistic view of human society. There is no reason why 'heroic' and 'individualistic' attitudes cannot coexist, and the truth is they did. The 'Epic Age' did not end with Homer. A great deal of epic poetry was recited and composed during the archaic period; in the fifth century tragedy perpetuated heroic values. Certainly the πόλις rose, and the aristocracies declined; but the ordinary citizen in the πόλις was just as interested in the heroes of old as were the aristocrats. It was the πόλις that built the hero-shrines, and a tyrant who organized the rhapsodic contests of the Panathenaea; not for nothing did the Greeks send for the Aiakides before the battle of Salamis.

Moreover, the πόλις did not come into existence after Homer; in his time the institution was well on its way to maturity. Its origins belong to an earlier period, to the renewal of culture after the Dark Ages. It was at that earlier time that epic too began to develop, long before it reached its peak in the late eighth and early seventh centuries.

4 To say that the *Iliad*, the *Odyssey*, Hesiod, and Archilochus represent four successive and self-contained stages of cultural development is to place an analytical straitjacket on historical change. It seems unlikely, perhaps impossible, that all the developments posited by the Fränkel-Snell school could have taken place in the time allotted (if we place Homer's *floruit* at, say, 725–700, and that of Archilochus at 680–40); but even if we grant that it is possible (since we have within our own experience a society which has changed with great speed), it is unlikely that all the many historical changes would be accurately reflected in the works of these poets, neatly organized into successive stages for our inspection. Things were probably more complicated than that. One might attempt to counter this objection by

saying that Homer to some extent looks backward, while Archilochus looks forward; but that would be to beg a question. There is much that is old in the *Iliad*, but to call the heroic view of life 'archaizing' is only possible by virtue of the theory; there is much also that is new. Homer and Archilochus were able to entertain their respective views of life while living roughly at the same time.

The chronology of the series is also uncertain. Several scholars have recently restated the case for thinking that Hesiod antedates Homer;[10] if this is true, all the cultural 'developments' traced in the poetry of Hesiod become questionable. Indeed, the *Odyssey* may well be contemporary with Archilochus.

5 Milman Parry has made us aware of the vast tradition behind Homer. Traditional epic phrases in Archilochus are not necessarily Homeric; they may have come, more likely did come, from other epic poetry. This possibility needs always to be kept in mind, and the 'imitations' judged accordingly.

Still, it is possible that by Archilochus' time, the poems of Homer existed more or less in their final form, and had through their excellence eclipsed the rest of the epic tradition. If so, it is more likely that parallels between seventh-century lyric and Homer are imitations, because the influence of the Homeric poems is, in this view, far greater than the influence of other epics. If lyric poets are imitating specific passages of a particular epic, there are obvious consequences for our understanding of their literary art. We can compare the model and the imitation, and draw appropriate conclusions. For followers of the Fränkel-Snell school, there are historical consequences as well; on the basis of the imitations, cultural and intellectual developments can be discovered.

The assumption that Homer's poems already represented the epic tradition for Archilochus and other seventh-century poets, as they do for us, rests in part on those very passages in lyric which are thought to imitate epic not only in their diction but also in the themes they borrow from Homer or Hesiod. Literary histories often claim that (for example) Archilochus fr 13 imitates *Iliad* 24.49, *Odyssey* 18.130ff, and other epic passages; that fr 134 imitates *Odyssey* 22.412; or that Tyrtaeus fr 11.31ff imitates *Iliad* 13.130f and/or 16.215. There are certainly some imitations of Homer in the lyric poets, yet many of these supposed instances are commonplaces, while others offer traditional sentiments from the store of Greek ethical wisdom, and still others express views in language which is purely natural or purely conventional in the given context.[11] One or two imitations, and the view that 'Homer' can be equated with 'the epic,' have led to the careless assumption that all parallels must be imitations. This view is confined neither to the

Fränkel-Snell school nor to modern times; but it has led modern theorists in particular to the unwarranted 'discovery' of all sorts of developments in the mental and social world of Lyric Age Greeks. It has led also to incorrect conclusions about the technique of μίμησις in the literature of the period. We read that a lyric poet's use of a single word is meant to recall whole passages in Homer; that the Homeric context is assumed as background, and necessary to the understanding of the lyric poem; that lyric poets combine a word from this book of Homer with a phrase from another and a line from a third. We read constantly of 'adaptations' of Homeric phrases. However, an analysis of the few certain cases of imitation reveals that this Virgilian description of the technique of early Greek lyric is inappropriate.

We are really dealing here with two questions: Did Homer's text exist in nearly final form in the early seventh century? Had it already eclipsed other epics, so that it was the principal representative of the epic tradition, as it is for us? An affirmative answer to the first does not imply an affirmative answer to the second. One or two certain examples of imitation in lyric do not guarantee that other, less certain examples also imitate Homer. Although Homer's eminence encouraged others to imitate him, poets throughout the archaic period continued to use traditional phrases to evoke the atmosphere of epic in a general sort of way. They needed no specific models; phrases came readily to their minds from the epics they heard everywhere about them.[12] This is, I think, a more reasonable view than that which traces everything to Homer; it is consistent with what evidence we have, and with our general knowledge of the epic tradition as it has been increased by Milman Parry.[13]

6 Finally, the theory fails to take account of the certainty that Archilochus had predecessors. It regards him as the πρῶτος εὑρετής of lyric; although Greeks sang songs before Archilochus, it argues that they were popular songs, lacking the art of that poet. The principal, quantifiable ingredient which sets Archilochus' lyric apart from ordinary song is the extensive use of epic diction; Archilochus, after all, had Homer and Hesiod behind him. Thus the Fränkel-Snell school can maintain that Archilochus, in restating or rejecting Homeric values, must use Homer's language, because he has no other model for composing high poetry.

We have argued above that 'epic' attitudes continued to be found after the end of the so-called 'Epic Age.' The converse is also true: 'lyric' attitudes were found before Archilochus. The work of the Indo-Europeanists has shown convincingly – as one might expect – that non-epic song was a part of Indo-European culture; details of the poetic language can be reconstructed.[14] Also helpful is K.J. Dover's examination of songs from pre-literate cultures;[15] among a number of interesting features shared by Archilochus is the expression of opinions and feelings in the first person (whether standing for the singer himself, the singer as a stock character, or the singer as a representative of the community). To express such feelings is the purpose of lyric, and when Archilochus says εἰμὶ δ' ἐγώ (fr 1.1), it is no evidence for the new importance of the individual, or the arrival of the 'Lyric Age.'

It is nonetheless true that the use of epic diction sets Archilochus and other lyric poets apart; but the significance of this fact is a matter of contention. Some scholars, it is true, have tried to deny or mitigate the fact, saying that part or all of what looks like epic in the lyric poets is not really epic. It will be convenient to discuss these arguments here. First is the view advanced by Dover, that we often have little idea of what was poetic and what vernacular in seventh-century Ionic.[16] Despite the objections of Page,[17] this view seems to me to have some force; many words, if they are found only in old Ionic and the epic, may indeed have been vernacular. Unfortunately, we have not the evidence to decide the issue; and many undoubtedly poetic words will remain in the lyric vocabulary. Secondly, some attempt might be made to revive the theory of August Fick, that the language of elegy was originally pure Ionic, not just epic stripped of its foreign elements,[18] and that non-dialectal features were first admitted in Mimnermus. If this view were adopted, it could be argued that elegy was essentially independent from epic in its early days, and that any shared vocabulary came from a high poetic language on which both had drawn. However, by no means all of Archilochus' epithets could be accounted for in this manner; for example, δουρικλυτοί (fr 3.5) must be epic. Furthermore, in order to maintain his view of the purity of the dialect in early elegy, Fick had to emend in a number of places; this is of course a petitio principii.[19] Third, it has been argued by several that the language of Homer, Hesiod, and the lyric poets goes back ultimately to a common base in the Mycenaean period, from which the different streams developed more or less independently.[20] Hesiod and the mainland elegists had their own traditions; their poetry only looks Ionic because scholars have overestimated the specifically Ionic contribution to the epic dialect, and because the poetry was transmitted through Athens, where many dialectal irregularities were smoothed out. If this argument were true, it would mean that artistic lyric – I emphasize, artistic, Archilochean lyric – was being composed all through the Dark Ages on the mainland, and presumably in Ionia as well; what we call the epic element in elegy is really just the common poetic language. This is, in a way, Fick's view with an added Mycenaean dimension. However, that Hesiod is not independent of Ionic epic has now been satisfactorily established;[21] and if Hesiod is not independent, neither is mainland elegy.[22] Fourth, it might be supposed that Archilochus is an oral poet, in the sense that he uses formulae within extended and economic systems. Now there is not enough of the work of Archilochus to detect systems in any event; and it will be shown below that the attempt to prove him an oral poet by comparing his poetry to the systems of Homer and Hesiod fails. But suppose for the moment that he is one; it would then be plausible to say that there was a non-epic tradition behind him, because systems have to evolve over a period of generations.[23] Most of Archilochus' epic-like phrases would not have come to him directly from epic, but from his own tradition. It may be that they were originally borrowed from the epic, but by the seventh century the debt had been forgotten. Lyric poets would have come to think that the high language was as much theirs as the epic poets' (the 'common stock' theory again). The multiplication of hypotheses in this view is unattractive; it is hard to believe, moreover, that phrases like μῶλον Ἄρης συνάγηι (Archil. fr 3.2) and scores of others in lyric had no epic flavour about them for poet or audience; and in any event Archilochus was no oral poet.

Initial impressions that the epic is important in the diction of early lyric are, then, correct; but the interpretation of its importance is, as I have said, another matter. Archilochus was not the first to distinguish his poems by using epic; at the same time as he was active in Paros and Thasos, Tyrtaeus in Sparta and Callinus in Ephesus were also composing elegy. Even if we were to grant that folk songs were of no importance for lyric, the advent of the 'Lyric Age' would have to be backdated at least one generation, perhaps more, to account for the simultaneous appearance of elegy in three locations.[24] But the generic elements – the types of subject-matter, the typical attitudes, the conventions – *were* given to Archilochus by his tradition.[25] He is expressing ideas which differ from those of epic; they are not thereby new. Following one or two or a dozen predecessors, he simply says what he has to say through the language of epic.[26] His epicisms are used judiciously, not slavishly, as A.E. Harvey observes.[27] Some forerunner of Archilochus had the good idea of using epic diction in a calculated way to achieve a more elevated tone; it was an excellent literary.device. There is no implication here that the poets were dependent on epic for other aspects of their art.

Some possible objections and issues of incidental relevance remain to be dealt with. One might naturally inquire why, if Archilochus had all these predecessors, we have no indication of their existence. Legend, it is true, provides us with the names of poets who, though they may not be historical, at least reflect an earlier tradition; this in itself is some kind of evidence for a pre-Archilochean 'Lyric Age.' However, these poets – Musaeus, Orpheus, Olen, etc – were all, so far as can be gathered, composers of heroic, religious or semi-religious poetry. No mythical ancestor is forthcoming for Archilochus' type of personal poetry.

The silence of the tradition is not surprising. It was not general practice in the eighth century to record poetry in writing;[28] therefore the works of earlier poets perished, and the preservation even of their names would depend on chance mention in the work of a later poet. Of course, if they were very famous, they would have been remembered by future generations; that we have no names encourages the idea that none were worth remembering. There are quantities of anonymous elegy from later periods, anonymous because composed by amateurs.

The argument that lyric poets of the eighth century have not been preserved because they could not or did not think to write their works down involves an assumption which needs examining: that such poems could not have been preserved by oral means. On the face of it this contention seems dubious, since we know that rhapsodes had no difficulty remembering much longer texts, and that folk songs do in fact undergo this treatment regularly. We all know songs by heart which we have learned from others, but have never seen in print. Greek examples are known.

Yet we can also point to numerous poets in archaic Greece – eg Clonas, Xenocritus, Polymnestus – of whom not a single word survives, and who were perhaps mere names already in the fifth century. By that time even Terpander's genuine works had probably perished; we have a few lines of Echembrotus only because he carved them on a tripod. It is plausible that these and other poets failed to record their works; if they did record them, they failed to see to the preservation of the manuscript. In any event, oral memory did nothing to keep their poetry alive, and we can believe that the work of Terpander at least would have been worth the effort of memorization.

The resolution of the dilemma is not hard to find. Popular songs are transmitted orally because they are capable of fulfilling their purpose again and again. A song often forms part of a specific type of social occasion, and newcomers learn it so that they may participate the next time the event takes place. The poems of Archilochus are not of this type; they are often tied to a particular, non-recurring event, and most of them are meant as art. They are of a distinctly higher order than any of the *carmina popularia* in PMG, or the primitive songs examined by Dover and Bowra. In Ruth Finnegan's wide-ranging book, there is no example of short *artistic* verse preserved by oral means.[29] We do know that the Greeks memorized the poems of the great lyric poets for singing at symposia; but whether this practice is as old as pre-Archilochean times is unknown. Certainly, the somewhat altered version of Alcaeus fr 249 which appears in PMG 891 tells against those who wish to say that, if Archilochus had predecessors, they could have been accurately preserved by oral means.[30]

A few general remarks, before I leave the theory of the Fränkel-Snell school. We used to think, quite naturally, that Greek civilization practically began with Homer. We now have to take into account a millennium or more of Greek history before him, even if much of this period remains obscure. Yet it is not easy to rid ourselves entirely of the notion that Homer stands at the beginning of a long line of development. This notion dominates the thinking of Fränkel and the others, no matter how willingly they may admit that *fuerunt ante Homerum poetae*. Because Homer must be 'stage one', there cannot *ex hypothesi* be much in him. It cannot be said strongly enough: Homer was no primitive. The fact is that he stands towards the *end* of the line.

In this respect, Hugh Lloyd-Jones, Snell's principal critic, is undoubtedly right. It is possible, of course, that he overstates his case; he quotes Dodds to that effect in his preface.[31] Yet his main point that scholars have been too concerned with tracing cultural developments is surely well taken. Human societies do of course develop; but in this case too many developments have been found, and they have been described in the wrong terms. The idea that human beings had to 'discover the mind' implies that they were once ignorant of individuality, and reflects outdated anthropological theory. To say that the succession of the 'Epic Age' by the 'Lyric Age' is revealed by lexicographical considerations, or by the modification of Homeric models in supposed lyric imitations, is on the one hand to make a large claim on the basis of limited evidence; yet on the other hand it is to fail to see the literature as part of a plausible historical context, a failure all the more surprising after the work of Wilamowitz.[32] Archaic literature by itself has been used to reconstruct the historical and social context; but it can be used only in conjunction with other evidence, and must itself be interpreted in the light of that evidence. The tradition offers us scattered information which points to a society more complex than the Fränkel-Snell school would have us believe. After the fall of Mycenae, Greece languished; then, under the influence of Near Eastern contacts, life began to stir. The πόλις was born; the arts grew and matured, poetry more quickly than others. Epic reached its peak in Ionia, and the other genres flourished alongside. With the advent of writing the Dark Ages were nearly over. We find around 700 a bustling and many-faceted society, no embryo but an ἔφηβος; there is very little lacking before it reaches manhood.

It would be pleasant now if we could move on to discuss the fragments themselves. But an important question suggested at the outset must be first be considered: the relevance of 'oral poetry' to our investigation of Homer and the lyric poets. Obviously if Archilochus uses 'Homeric' or epic phrases as an oral epic poet uses his formulae, it will affect our understanding of

Archilochus' literary art. A Homeric phrase which we had thought was being used fairly precisely to achieve a certain effect would have to be considered rather as a formula, employed partly or mainly because it is the phrase required for that particular point in the line.

D.L. Page, indeed, argued that Archilochus, at least in his elegies, was an oral poet; in those epodes with a dactylic component, and to a greater extent in the iambic poems, Page thought that Archilochus was exploring a new, written technique.[33] This view has not found general assent, although one of Parry's followers eagerly proclaimed it.[34] In fact there are obvious deficiencies in Page's argument. As both Kirk and Dihle pointed out, he has not examined the nature and technique of the formula in sufficient detail.[35] For him, any word in Archilochus which also occurred in Homer, and any phrase which resembled a Homeric one, was a formula; and if there were enough of these, Archilochus was an oral poet. Clearly many questions have been avoided. If, however, one were to begin with a more satisfactory understanding of the formula and the technique of improvisation, it might be possible to prove Page's thesis.

Immediately one encounters theoretical and methodological difficulties. In the field of Homeric studies, problems such as the definition of the formula and the nature of the formula-system are far from being solved to the satisfaction of everyone; in deciding whether Archilochus was an oral poet, further problems are encountered. In the first place, not nearly enough poetry of Archilochus (or of any early lyric poet) survives to allow the detection of the formula-systems which are an essential part of oral improvisation. Strictly speaking, the proposition can never be proven, and the investigation should be called to a halt before it has even begun; but most will want a more satisfactory solution than this.

Since systems cannot be discovered, the case for orality must be proved from the sheer quantity of formulae in Archilochus. Which phrases qualify as formulae would have to be decided on the basis of comparison with the systems of Homer and Hesiod.[36] Yet this method, too, is not without its difficulties. Dihle and others have insisted on a strict definition of the formula in Homer: a phrase must be repeated in the same form in the same part of the verse if it is to be so designated.[37] At the most, modifications in case-endings might be allowed (eg Ποσειδάωνος ἄνακτος/Ποσειδάωνι ἄνακτι), so long as the metrical structure remained unchanged. On this definition, the formularity of Homer would have to be drastically reduced. A similar reduction in Archilochus would result. For the only phrases with exact parallels in epic are fr 5.3 (v.l.) θανάτου τέλος (Hes. Op. 166), fr 13.3 κῦμα πολυφλοίσβοιο θαλάσσης (eg Il. 2.209, 6.347), fr 1.1 Ἐννναλίοιο ἄνακτος ([Hes.] Sc. 371), and fr 12 Ποσειδάωνος ἄνακτος (Il. 20.67).[38]

The first is a variant, perhaps resulting from an imperfect recollection of Homer; the other three are very much the sort of phrase a lettered poet might use if he were aiming for epic effect; and the last two owe as much to religious language as to the epic.

Realizing the consequences of a strict definition, followers of Parry seek to increase the percentage of formulae in Homer by using the concepts of 'formula-systems' and 'formulaic language.'[39] A.B. Lord, for example, maintains that in a formula-system, one word in a phrase remains constant, while the other may be replaced by any word of the same metrical shape:

$$\left.\begin{array}{l} \mathring{a}\lambda\gamma\varepsilon' \\ \kappa\hat{v}\delta\sigma\varsigma \\ \tau\varepsilon\acute{v}\chi\varepsilon' \\ \varepsilon\mathring{v}\nu\iota\nu \end{array}\right\} \ \ \ \ddot{\varepsilon}\theta\eta\kappa\varepsilon$$

Even though the phrase εὖνιν ἔθηκε occurs only once in the Iliad (22.44), it can be called 'formulaic' because it belongs to this system. Structure, in this view, has as much importance as semantics, and it was only to be expected that someone would take the step of asserting that both words in a phrase can be replaced.[40] We find definitions of the formula such as 'any verb plus direct object in the shape -$\upsilon\upsilon$--.' Hainsworth objects to structuralist views of the formula, and emphasizes the flexibility of the formula in his own definition of the formula-system.[41] He points out that the purpose of the formula is to allow the poet to fill in spaces of varying lengths created as the spontaneous performance proceeds. The outstanding feature of oral technique is not therefore the memorization and combination of a vast number of existing, rigid formulae, but the fluid adaptation of a smaller number of formulae to meet immediate requirements. This process is visible when we compare with each other such Homeric phrases as:

τὸν δ' αὖτε προσέειπε / τὸν δ' ἀπαμειβόμενος προσέφη / τὸν δ' ἀπαμειβό-μενος προσεφώνεε

or

διογενὴς Ὀδυσσεύς / Ὀδυσσεὺς δουρικλυτός / πολύτλας δῖος Ὀδυσσεύς / πολύ-μητις Ὀδυσσεύς / δῖος Ὀδυσσεύς.

It is groups of phrases such as these, where the members of the group are similar in meaning, which Hainsworth terms 'formula-systems.' Among the different types of formulaic modification are mobility within the line, modification of case-endings (with or without change of metrical shape), reversal of word-order, the combination of two existing formulae, the expansion of formulae by the insertion of extra adjectives, and the 'separation' or splitting up of formulae.

Some of the concepts involved in the theory of the Homeric formula might be applied to lyric poetry. The ways in which formulae are modified within the Homeric corpus might be said to be analogous to the ways in which Archilochus has 'adapted' his phrases from Homer and Hesiod. This is a hazardous assumption, and probably raises more questions than it answers; but it is the only one available if one is to assert with some show of reason that more phrases in Archilochus are formulae than those which have exact parallels in the epic. Of course, if Archilochus was an oral poet, he would, like Hesiod, have had many unique formulae. The surviving fragments might contain an unrepresentative number of such formulae; but only slight allowance can be made for this possibility. Archilochus' orality, in short, might not be entirely obvious; but his literacy should be.[42]

Below is a list of phrases[43] from the elegies of Archilochus, and from the dactylic lines of the epodes,[44] which are candidates for the degree and status of formula. The criteria used are as follows. I have excluded phrases like τοίους γάρ and ἀλλὰ τάχιστα, even if they are paralleled in the same part of the verse, since such phrases include connectives and are rarely part of a formulaic system even in Homer.[45] I have also excluded phrases made up of perfectly ordinary words (e.g. ἐπὶ τόξα τανύσσεται, fr 3.1),[46] unless the whole phrase is found in the same position in the epic. Conversely, if a phrase is made up of epic words, it is included even if none of the words is attested in the same position; no limit is placed on the degree of flexibility. Phrases in which one word is paralleled in the same part of the verse illustrate a straightforward type of flexibility and are included. If one word of a phrase recurs in the same part of the verse, but a different word has been substituted for the second part of the epic formula, the phrase is included if the substituted word is semantically related to its epic counterpart (eg ἀσπίδι ... ἀγάλλεται, fr 5.1; see below). For pentameters, I have allowed phrases which are found both at the beginning of the hemiepes and the beginning of epic hexameters, or at the end of the hemiepes and before the masculine or hephthemimeral caesura. Phrases from the hemiepes which with slight alteration (eg -oιο for -oυ) would fit the end of a hexameter are allowed (no 38). Phrases recurring in the same or similar form in the pentameters of other elegists are dubbed 'pentameter formulae' and permitted as evidence of oral composition. In epodes with a dactylic component, verse-end formulae occurring before the rhythm changes are listed; also listed is a phrase found at the end of the dactylic run of the epode and before the bucolic diaeresis of an epic hexameter (no 32). Phrases from pentameters and epodes which do not meet these stipulations are given in parentheses. In brief, the allowance made for error is very generous. Very few epic-sounding phrases have been excluded.[47]

1 Fr 1.1 θεράπων ... Ἐνναλίοιο ἄνακτος. θεράπων Ἄρηος is an epic phrase (eg Il. 7.382, 19.47); θεράπων in the same position with other deities: Od. 11.255, Hes. Th. 100, Margites fr 1.2, hHom. 32.20 (the last three with the Muses). Ἐνναλίοιο ἄνακτος is found in the same position in [Hes.] Sc. 371.

2 Fr 1.2 Μουσέων ... ἐρατὸν δῶρον. The expression 'gift of the gods' is very common; for the Muses, cf Hes. Th. 103, 93, Alcm. PMG 59(b) 1f, Theog. 250, Anac. fr eleg 2.3. ἐρατός is a favourite lyric adjective; perhaps then this expression is a 'pentameter formula.' (ἐρατόν with δῶρον is not regular epic, as Page asserts, Archiloque 134; only Il. 3.64, δῶρ' ἐρατὰ ... Ἀφροδίτης. AP 6.346.2 = Anac. fr dub 196.2 Gentili offers ἀντ' ἐρατῶν δώρων.)

3 Fr 2.2 ἐν δορὶ κεκλιμένος. Cf Il. 3.135 ἀσπίσι κεκλιμένοι, Od. 6.307 κίονι κεκλιμένη (both before the masculine caesura). The ἐν of Archilochus' expression is not paralleled, and it is this word which has given interpreters most difficulty.

4 Fr 3.1f θαμειαί / σφενδόναι. The adjective occurs (not with σφενδόνη) at the end of the line at Il. 1.52, 12.44, etc; the noun occurs in the dative at the beginning of the line at Il. 13.600.

5 Fr 3.2 (μῶλον Ἄρης συνάγηι) is included because μῶλος Ἄρηος and συνάγειν Ἄρηα / μῶλον Ἄρηος (also ὑσμίνην and φύλοπιν) are such common expressions in epic; comparison with the pentameters of other elegists is of little help, and the expression in Archilochus (where Ares is the subject) reverses the epic manner.

6 Fr 3.3 ξιφέων ... πολύστονον ἔργον. Cf Il. 6.522 ἔργον ... μάχης, 11.734 ἔργον Ἄρηος, Hes. Op. 146 ἔργα ... στονόεντα. πολύστονος: Il. 15.451.

7 Fr 3.4 (δάμονες ... μάχης): Il. 5.634 μάχης ἀδαήμονι, 13.811 μάχης ἀδαήμονες.

8 Fr 3.5 δεσπόται ... δουρικλυτοί: δουρικλυτός occurs always in this part of the verse in Homer; the noun is not attested, but δέσποινα (Od. 3.403 etc) and δεσπόσυνος (hCer. 144) are epic.

9 Fr 4.6 θοῆς διὰ σέλματα νηός. 'Fast ship' is standard epic diction (no parallel for this part of the verse); σέλματα is found in the same position at hHom. 7.47.

10 Fr 4.6f διὰ σέλματα νηὸς / φοίτα. The verb at the beginning of the

verse (though as an imperfect) occurs at *Il.* 5.595 etc; *Od.* 12.420 ἐγὼ διὰ νηὸς ἐφοίτων.

11 Fr 4.8 οἶνον ἐρυθρόν. A verse-end formula (*Od.* 5.165 etc), it is not attested in this part of the verse.

12 Fr 5.1 ἀσπίδι ... ἀγάλλεται. The verb is found in the same position at *Il.* 17.473 and 18.132, both times in conjunction with weapons.

13 Fr 5.2 (ἐντὸς ἀμώμητον): the adjective is used of persons in epic and lyric (once in tragedy); perhaps an ordinary word in old Ionic. Elsewhere it is always plural; Archilochus uses the singular also at fr 139.5.

14 Fr 5.3 (v.l.) ἐξέφυγεν ... θανάτου τέλος. The last two words occur in the same part of the verse at Hes. *Op.* 166; variants of the expression (ἐκ)φυγεῖν θάνατον may be found at *Il.* 11.362, 20.350, 449, *Od.* 16.21.

15 Fr 6 (ξείνια λυγρά): for the noun, see, for example, *Od.* 9.356; the adjective is frequent in epic with a variety of nouns, but is not attested with this one.

16 Fr 8.1 πολιῆς ἁλὸς ἐν πελάγεσσι. πολιῆς ἁλός (eg *Il.* 1.359) and ἁλὸς ἐν πελάγεσσι (*hHom.* 33.15, *hAp.* 73) are both found in the same part of the verse.

17 Fr 8.2 θεσσάμενοι (γλυκερὸν νόστον). The participle is found at the beginning of the verse in Hes. fr 231; for the remainder cf *Od.* 22.323 νόστοιο τέλος γλυκεροῖο.

18 Fr 9.10 (χαρίεντα μέλεα): cf *Il.* 16.798 χαρίεν τε μέτωπον, *Il.* 18.24, *hHom.* 31.12 χαρίεν ... πρόσωπον, *Il.* 22.402f κάρη ... χαρίεν.

19 Fr 9.11 καθαροῖσιν ἐν εἵμασιν: *Od.* 6.61, 4.750 = 17.48 καθαρὰ ... εἵματα.

20 Fr 13.1 κήδεα μὲν στονόεντα: *Il.* 1.445 πολύστονα κήδεα, *Od.* 9.12 κήδεα ... στονόεντα.

21 Fr 13.2 (θαλίης τέρψεται): *Od.* 11.603 τέρπεται ἐν θαλίης, Hes. *Op.* 115 τέρποντ' ἐν θαλίηισι.

22 Fr 13.3f κῦμα ... ἔκλυσεν: cf *hAp.* 74f ἔνθ' ἐμὲ μὲν μέγα κῦμα κατὰ κρατὸς ἅλις αἰεὶ / κλύσσει.

23 Fr 13.5 ἀνηκέστοισι ... κακοῖσιν: Hes. *Th.* 612 ἀνήκεστον κακόν.

24 Fr 13.7 ἄλλοτε ἄλλος: *Il.* 15.684 ἄλλοτ' ἐπ' ἄλλον (same position); cf Sol. fr 13.43 ἄλλοθεν ἄλλος (same position).

25 Fr 13.8 (αἱματόεν ἕλκος): the adjective is in the epic at *Il.* 2.267 (σμῶδιξ), 9.650, 19.313 (πόλεμος); the whole phrase could be ordinary Ionic.

26 Fr 13.10 πένθος ἀπωσάμενοι: *Il.* 12.276 νεῖκος ἀπωσαμένους (at beginning of verse), *hCer.* 276 γῆρας ἀπωσαμένη (at beginning of verse).

27 Fr 14.2 μάλα πόλλ' ... πάθοι: *Il.* 9.492 μάλα πόλλ' ἔπαθον (μάλα πόλλ' before masculine caesura); *Od.* 2.174 κακὰ πολλὰ παθόντα, 13.90 μάλα πολλὰ πάθ' ἄλγεα.

28 Fr 168.3 πολὺ φίλταθ᾽ ἑταίρων. φίλταθ᾽ ἑταίρων occurs at verse-end *Il.* 13.249, 19.315; πολὺ φίλταθ᾽ ἑταίρων at verse-end *Od.* 24.517 (cf *Il.* 24.748 πάντων πολὺ φίλτατε παίδων). πολὺ φίλτατος is an established formula.

29 Fr 169 χεῖρας ἀνέξων. χεῖρας ἀνέσχον is found at verse-end, *Il.* 3.318; cf 6.257, 301 etc; elsewhere in the verse *Il.* 8.347, 24.301 etc. (The formula is not actually attested with ἀνέξων.)

30 Fr 185.4 μοῦνος ἀν᾽ ἐσχατίην. μοῦνος comes frequently at the beginning of the line; ἐπ᾽ ἐσχατίην (*Od.* 24.150) and ἐπ᾽ ἐσχατίηι (*Od.* 2.391, 9.182, 10.96, Hes. *Th.* 622) are found before the masculine caesura.

31 Fr 185.6 πυκνὸν ἔχουσα νόον. In epic cf *Il.* 15.461 πυκινὸν νόον, 24.282 = 674 πυκινὰ μήδε᾽ ... ἔχοντες, etc; the phrase may count as a 'pentameter formula,' cf Theog. 74, 580, 792, and below pp 43ff.

32 Fr 188 (SLG 478b) 1 ἁπαλὸν χρόα. The phrase is now attested in the *Meropis* fr 3.3, before the bucolic diaeresis.[48] Hes. *Op.* 519, hVen. 14, Theog. 1341 have the adjective ἁπαλόχρως. ἁπαλός is frequently used with parts of the body in epic and lyric. (Line 3, γλυκὺς ἵμερος: cf eg *Il.* 3.139, 446; 14.328; *Od.* 22.500.)

33 Fr 190 (καὶ βήσσας ὀρέων †δυσπαιπάλους): *Il.* 3.34 etc οὔρεος ἐν βήσσηις, 13.17 ἐξ ὄρεος ... παιπαλόεντος, 17.743 ἐξ ὄρεος κατὰ παιπαλόεσσαν ἀταρπόν.

34 Fr 191.3 (κλέψας ... ἁπαλὰς [ἀταλάς cj Meineke] φρένας): *Il.* 14.217 ἔκλεψε νόον; 6.400 ἀταλάφρονα, 11.115 ἁπαλόν ... ἦτορ ἀπηύρα, 18.567 ἀταλὰ φρονέοντες; cf hCer. 24, Hes. *Th.* 989.

35 Fr 193.2 χαλεπῆισι ... ὀδύνηισιν: hAp. 358 ὀδύνηισιν ... χαλεπῆισι. (2f ὀδύνηισιν ... πεπαρμένος: cf *Il.* 5.399, hAp. 92.)

36 Fr 195 οἴκαδ᾽ ἄγεσθαι: *Il.* 3.404, *Od.* 10.35, hHom. 6.17 (at verse-end); cf *Il.* 3.72, *Od.* 21.316, Hes. *Op.* 695.

37 The Cologne Epode line 7 (εἶδος ἄμωμον): Hes. *Th.* 259 εἶδος ἄμωμος.

38 The Cologne Epode line 19 πείσομαι ὥς με κέλεαι: *Il.* 23.96 πείσομαι ὡς σὺ κελεύεις (at verse-end).

Counting the dactylic metron as two elements (an element being either a long or two shorts), we obtain the following percentages of formular and formulaic diction in Archilochus' verses. For the novice in this kind of analysis, the figure of 33 per cent for the hexameters means that on average one-third of each hexameter contains epic formulae or formulaic expressions.

1 Hexameters            33%
2 Pentameters, including phrases in parentheses        34%
3 Pentameters, excluding phrases in parentheses        20%
4 Elegy, including phrases in parentheses        33.3%

5   Elegy, excluding phrases in parentheses        28%
6   Dactylic components of epodes        24%
7   As no 6, excluding phrases in parentheses        17%
8   Elegy and epodes together, including phrases in parentheses        30%
9   As no 8, excluding phrases in parentheses        24%

These figures cannot support the conclusion that Archilochus was an oral poet. When one considers that most of each percentage is made up of a 'formulaic' component, the case is even clearer; phrases with exactly parallel positions in epic account for only 12 per cent of the hexameters, 7 per cent of elegy.[49] The quantity of formulae is not impressive, even if the phrases in parentheses, which do not meet the stipulations made at the outset for adapted formulae, are included. The plea that unrepresentative evidence has concealed both the complete number of formulae and the existence of systems is not convincing. If we had all the poetry of Archilochus, as well as that of his predecessors and lost contemporaries, the figures would not increase dramatically. We have sufficient later elegy to compare one poet with another, and find no more formularity in them than we do in Archilochus. It might be argued, of course, that they have all become literate poets in the meantime; but their technique of using epic diction selectively is exactly the same as Archilochus'. The number of formulae is one consideration; the way they are used is another. No reader of Archilochus can think that these phrases are employed as they are in epic. They are precisely chosen; there is hardly an example of a purely ornamental epithet, and perhaps not one is used incongruously.[50]

We can now evaluate the presence of epic in lyric poetry from a literary point of view. I propose to consider first the use lyric poets make of particular passages, and then the use of the epic language in general. For borrowings of content, the main literary question is the technique of imitation, μίμησις: to what use are the original models put in their new contexts, and what is the nature of any changes made? Below I consider many passages which have been or could be claimed as borrowings from the epic; at the same time as we address the problem of imitation, we must also decide which passages are even relevant.[51]

EPIC PASSAGES IMITATED IN LYRIC POETRY

Seventh Century

1   Archilochus fr 13.5–10

ἀλλὰ θεοὶ γὰρ ἀνηκέστοισι κακοῖσιν
ὦ φίλ᾽ ἐπὶ κρατερὴν τλημοσύνην ἔθεσαν

φάρμακον. ἄλλοτε ἄλλος ἔχει τόδε· νῦν μὲν ἐς ἡμέας
ἐτράπεθ᾽, αἱματόεν δ᾽ ἕλκος ἀναστένομεν,
ἐξαῦτις δ᾽ ἑτέρους ἐπαμείψεται. ἀλλὰ τάχιστα
τλῆτε, γυναικεῖον πένθος ἀπωσάμενοι.

Compare:

τλητὸν γὰρ Μοῖραι θυμὸν θέσαν ἀνθρώποισιν.

(Il. 24.49)

ἀτὰρ θεὸς ἄλλοτε ἄλλωι
Ζεὺς ἀγαθόν τε κακόν τε διδοῖ.

(Od. 4.236f)

Ζεὺς δ᾽ αὐτὸς νέμει ὄλβον Ὀλύμπιος ἀνθρώποισιν,
ἐσθλοῖς ἠδὲ κακοῖσιν, ὅπως ἐθέλῃσιν, ἑκάστωι.
καί που σοὶ τάδ᾽ ἔδωκε, σὲ δὲ χρὴ τετλάμεν ἔμπης.

(Od. 6.188–90)

ἀλλ᾽ ὅτε δὴ καὶ λυγρὰ θεοὶ μάκαρες τελέσωσι,
καὶ τὰ φέρει ἀεκαζόμενος τετληότι θυμῶι.

(Od. 18.134–5)

ἄλλοτε δ᾽ ἀλλοῖος Ζηνὸς νόος αἰγιόχοιο,
ἀργαλέος δ᾽ ἄνδρεσσι καταθνητοῖσι νοῆσαι.
εἰ δέ κεν ὄψ᾽ ἀρόσῃς, τόδε κέν τοι φάρμακον εἴη.

(Hes. Op. 483–5)

The Archilochean passage shows no verbal similarity to the others close enough to suggest dependence; there is however a similarity of content. Many additional passages could be cited to show the idea that the blessings of life are inconstant (the *locus classicus* is *Il.* 24.527ff) and that a 'remedy' is needed. In the passage of Hesiod cited above the 'remedy' is timely ploughing (486ff). τλημοσύνη is frequently the 'remedy' in lyric; the word, rare in any event, is lacking in Homer, but the concept is the same at *Odyssey*, 18.130–7 (see further below on frr 131–2). It is significant that in the one epic passage where τλημοσύνη occurs, *hAp.* 191, the context is the inevitability of death for men; so too at *Il.* 24.49, where we have only τλητὸν ... θυμόν.

An objection that can be levelled against many supposed lyric imitations of Homer immediately emerges. The content here is an item in the storehouse of traditional Greek wisdom; where so many parallel passages can be cited, the possibility is very strong that the idea was already commonplace in the time of Homer and Archilochus. Of course, Homer may have first stated the idea or given it a form that invited imitation; this probably happened in one of the passages discussed below (see p 32, cf p 27 on Archilochus frr 131–2). If, in one or two cases, the content of both model and copy were commonplace, then there would be no reason to doubt their dependence. But where, as we shall see, so many passages are commonplaces, reference to the general values of the society and common poetic property is probably sufficient to explain the similarities between lyric and epic. In these circumstances the burden of proof must rest with those who wish to prove borrowing. In the present passage, borrowing cannot be assumed in the absence of any close or extensive verbal parallels.[52]

2   Archilochus fr 110

†ἔρξω· ἐτήτυμον γὰρ ξυνὸς ἀνθρώποις Ἄρης.

Compare Il. 18.309:

ξυνὸς Ἐνυάλιος· καί τε κτανέοντα κατέκτα.

This and the next four examples are cited by Clement of Alexandria as instances of Archilochean imitation. The content is, again, commonplace; the gnomic form is particularly clear in Homer (omission of the copula, generalizing τε, gnomic aorist).

3   Archilochus fr 111

καὶ νέους θάρσυνε· νίκης δ' ἐν θεοῖσι πείρατα.

Compare Il. 7.102:

νίκης πείρατ' ἔχονται ἐν ἀθανάτοισι θεοῖσι.

The quotation of Homer is garbled in Clement (Strom. 6.6.1), but it seems this is the line he intended. It is a commonplace to say that something depends on the gods, or lies in their lap; in Archilochus, the thought has a gnomic form, though a verb may have followed in the next line. The verbal similarity is to some extent inevitable, and the periphrasis πείρατα / πεῖραρ plus genitive is common with various nouns.

4   Archilochus fr 127

ἤμβλακον· καί πού τιν' ἄλλον ἤδ' †ἄτη 'κιχήσατο.

Compare *Il.* 9.116:

ἀασάμην, οὐδ' αὐτὸς ἀναίνομαι.

It is doubtful that ἄτη can in any way be retained; Meineke's ἡ ἀάτη will do it, but the uncontracted form is unlikely, especially in combination with synekphonesis. If ἄτη is removed, then the similarity is non-existent; there are many contexts in which a person might admit to being wrong. But even with ἄτη, the point is scarcely surprising (see eg *Il.* 19.91ff, Solon fr 13.67f, Theognis 133f, Aesch. *Ag.* 385f). Some think that *Il.* 19.91ff is the real model, and that the parallel lies in the use both speakers make of ἄτη as an excuse (or at least as an explanation). However, in view of the passages just cited, we may be sure that any Greek of the period could have explained his aberrations in this way.

5  Archilochus fr 130. According to H. Kahn and others, this fragment imitates the proem to Hesiod's *Works and Days*.[53] The two passages have nothing in common, save that the gods can easily reverse men's fortunes, which is commonplace (below, n 80).

6  Archilochus fr 134

οὐ γὰρ ἐσθλὰ κατθανοῦσι κερτομεῖν ἐπ' ἀνδράσιν.

Compare *Od.* 22.412:

οὐχ ὁσίη κταμένοισιν ἐπ' ἀνδράσιν εὐχετάασθαι.

The content is gnomic; γάρ shows that the commonplace, typically, is being used to support an argument. One of Solon's laws was [ὁ νόμος] ὁ κωλύων ... τὸν τεθνηκότα κακῶς ἀγορεύειν (*Plut. Sol.* 21). Later parallels include Cratinus fr 102 Kassel-Austin and Euripides *Electra* 900ff.

7  Archilochus fr 25.2

ἀλλ' ἄλλος ἄλλωι καρδίην ἰαίνεται.

Compare *Od.* 14.228:

ἄλλος γάρ τ' ἄλλοισιν ἀνὴρ ἐπιτέρπεται ἔργοις.

There is nothing remarkable about this sentiment; in the *Odyssey* it is used in the gnomic manner as an explanation. Clement provides a parallel from

Euripides (fr 560 N²). καρδίην ἰαίνεται is a phrase borrowed from general epic stock (cf *Od.* 4.548f, *hCer.* 65, 435).

8  Archilochus fr 119

καὶ πεσεῖν δρήστην ἐπ᾽ ἀσκόν, κἀπὶ γαστρὶ γαστέρα
προσβαλεῖν, μηρούς τε μηροῖς.

Compare Tyrtaeus fr 11.31ff, *Il.* 13.130f, 16.215. Here we are confronted with a rather more specific idea and turn of expression than we have met in the other examples. Nonetheless it would be hasty to claim that Archilochus and Tyrtaeus are imitating Homer. It is natural to say 'man to man, sword to sword' when either describing close fighting, as Homer does, or urging men to fight closely, as Tyrtaeus does (compare further Archilochus fr 128.2f, Tyrt. fr 10.15, fr 11.4, 11f, 29, 38, fr 12.12, fr 19.13;[54] Eur. *Heracl.* 836f, *Hel.* 1072; Ar. *Vesp.* 1083). Callinus, when he thinks of close fighting, thinks in the same moment of individual pieces of gear: 'Let a man raise up his spear, gather his courage behind his shield and advance to close quarters, when battle is first joined.' (fr 1.9ff). Similarly Archilochus fr 3.1–3 (cf Ar. *Vesp.* 1081, Theocr. 22.65). Expressions like 'man to man, sword to sword' may already have been traditional in martial exhortations by Tyrtaeus' time. It is not surprising that a similar expression occurs in the Berlin papyrus (fr 19.15: ἀσπίδας εὐκύκλους ἀσπίσι τυπτ[ομεν-). But even if Tyrtaeus draws his inspiration from epic in these places, the formulaic repetition of the Homeric passage in two different books suggests that such descriptions of fighting were traditional in epic as well. Tyrtaeus could therefore have drawn on his general knowledge of epic as easily as on these two passages in Homer.

Archilochus too could have heard this mannerism in a dozen places – whether from epic or other poems like Tyrtaeus' – before he decided to give it a novel application. On the other hand, there are many examples of the same turn of phrase, quite naturally, in erotic contexts (eg Anac. *PMG* 439, Ovid *Am.* 1.4.43, 3.7.10; further parallels in Diehl's note on Tyrt. 11 [8 Diehl] 31ff); the possibility that it was already conventional in that genre as well cannot be ruled out.

9  Archilochus fr 128 (θυμὲ θύμ᾽ ἀμηχάνοισι κήδεσιν κυκώμενε). This fragment has been claimed as an imitation of *Od.* 20.18ff.[55] No word for endurance occurs in Archilochus' poem, but the idea is clearly present, as comparison with Theognis 1029–34 shows. This latter passage is in fact a closer parallel to Archilochus than the Homeric one, for it has also the idea 'neither *exult* nor grieve excessively' (expressing both sides of the situation, whereas Homer speaks only of the one aspect appropriate to his context). The motif of self-address alone cannot establish a connection between Archilo-

chus and Homer (or Archilochus and Theognis); it is an old device, a literary convention used throughout antiquity.[56] Its origins could lie in epic, since expressions like εἶπε πρὸς ὃν μεγαλήτορα θυμόν strike one as epic stylization; but Archilochus could just as well have known it from epics other than those of Homer. For 'endurance' as a commonplace, see above p 20ff on fr 13.5–10.

10  Archilochus fr 191

τοῖος γὰρ φιλότητος ἔρως ὑπὸ καρδίην ἐλυσθεὶς
πολλὴν κατ' ἀχλὺν ὀμμάτων ἔχευεν
κλέψας ἐκ στηθέων ἀπαλὰς φρένας.

Each line has been thought to imitate a different Homeric passage. ἐλυσθεὶς in line 1 suggests an imitation of *Od.* 9.433, where Odysseus is curled up beneath the ram's belly. Line 2 is taken from *Il.* 5.696:

τὸν δὲ λίπε ψυχή, κατὰ δ' ὀφθαλμῶν κέχυτ' ἀχλύς

and other lines (*Il.* 16.344, 20.321, 421) where the expression is used of death. Line 3 is inspired by a line from the Διὸς ἀπάτη in which πάρφασις is one of the charms Hera obtained from Aphrodite:

ἥ τ' ἔκλεψε νόον πύκα περ φρονεόντων

(*Il.* 14.217).[57]

Although it must remain a matter of judgment, it seems to me that ἐλυσθεὶς in the first line is not sufficient to point the way to a specific passage. The image of Odysseus 'coiled under the ram's belly' is striking, and so is the image of love 'coiled under the heart'; but can 'coiled under' in itself establish the connection? Similarly, the third line, κλέψας ἐκ στηθέων φρένας is admittedly closer to ἔκλεψε νόον πύκα φρονεόντων than the first line is to its alleged model, but perhaps not close enough to signal unambiguously a particular model.[58] Nor can the phrase ἀπαλαὶ (or ἀταλαὶ) φρένες do so, since it comes from the language of epic in general. Note too the gnomic form of the line in Homer; the capacity of love to deceive its victims is already traditional.

The second line is different; here everyone can recognize a phrase commonly used in epic to describe the experience of death. That is precisely the point, however; it is a phrase from epic poetry in general. Archilochus compares himself to a dying hero, as critics have pointed out; but we are not justified in finding psychological subtleties in the poem. To describe the effects of love as a confusion of the mind, a disruption of the senses, and an infliction of physical pain is common in erotic poetry of the period; reference to Archil. fr 193, Sappho fr 1.3f, fr 31.5ff, and Anac. PMG 413 will suffice. Archilochus has here combined this type of description with an epic turn of phrase, in keeping with other standard features of love poetry: a grand tone, impossible conceits, forceful language, and ironic self-deprecation. For the irony, we need only mention that δηὖτε is a conventional word in the context, often with a resigned or self-mocking tone.⁵⁹ For the conceits and forceful language we may cite: Archil. fr 193.2f ὀδύνηισιν ... πεπαρμένος δι' ὀστέων; the convention of 'riding' as a metaphor for love, particularly vigorous in Anac. PMG 360.3f (οὐκ εἰδὼς ὅτι τῆς ἐμῆς / ψυχῆς ἡνιοχεύεις); PMG 376, where Anacreon claims to have thrown himself off the White Rocks – again; the same fragment, where he says he is drunk with love; PMG 358.1f, where Eros physically strikes him with his ball; PMG 378, where the poet flies to Olympus; PMG 396, where he boxes with Eros; PMG 398, where the dice of Eros are madness and uproar; PMG 413, where Eros strikes him like a smith with an axe and plunges him in an ice-cold river. Ibycus PMG 286.10f Κύπριδος ἀζαλέαις μανίαισιν, and for less spectacular examples (the party-goers of the Theognidea are not all Anacreons), Theognis 1231, 1273f, 1306f, 1335 (γυμνάζεσθαι for making love), 1337 ἀπελάκτισ' ἀνίας, 1357f, 1361 may also be cited.⁶⁰ Archilochus' manner throughout is ironic, or, as Harvey says, 'mock-heroic'. ὑπὸ καρδίην ἐλυσθείς is remarkable for the concrete manner in which Archilochus thinks of his emotion, as a huddled, knotted lump in his midriff. The allusion to death in the second line is a conceit; the third line is quite melodramatic.

Two conclusions about the technique of μίμησις follow. First, imitation does not depend on the precise recall of particular passages; the reader is not required to compare the 'model' word for word in order to grasp the point. Secondly, the poet does not sit down with his text of the Iliad and take a word from this passage, a phrase from that, a line from another. The epic language in general is in the back of his mind, exerting an influence of which the poet is half conscious; he may have one or two particular passages in the front of his mind. Although his technique is no longer formular, it is not yet so precise that he wants the mot juste at every turn.⁶¹ The borrowing works in a loose way. Archilochus uses epic language to suggest the idea 'epic hero dying.' He does not mean 'as in Iliad 5.696'; nor does he then complicate things further by adducing two more passages; still less does he do so on the basis of a single word or phrase.

11   Archilochus frr 131–2⁶²

τοῖος ἀνθρώποισι θυμός, Γλαῦκε Λεπτίνεω πάϊ,
γίνεται θνητοῖς, ὁποίην Ζεὺς ἐφ' ἡμέρην ἄγει,
καὶ φρονέουσι τοῖ' ὁποίοις ἐγκυρέωσιν ἔργμασιν.

Compare *Od.* 18.136f:

τοῖος γὰρ νόος ἐστὶν ἐπιχθονίων ἀνθρώπων
οἷον ἐπ' ἦμαρ ἄγῃσι πατὴρ ἀνδρῶν τε θεῶν τε.

The idea that men are ἐφήμεροι is common in lyric, as well it might be, given the occasion it often has to speak of personal difficulties and grievances. The entire passage *Od.* 18.129–42 shows how 'lyric' sentiments can appear in epic. Again, we are dealing with a piece of traditional wisdom; but here the commonplace is given a particular expression in both passages. This situation is unlikely to be coincidental.[63]

It is perfectly possible that Homer is the imitator. Which way the imitation goes cannot, however, be determined, unless one looks very hard for clues that are not there, or brings the presuppositions of the Fränkel-Snell school to the discussion.[64] A straightforward reading suggests that there is no special significance in the change from (or to) θυμός, or in the addition (or subtraction) of Archilochus' third line. The borrowing is shown by extended verbal agreement on the one hand, but on the other the adaptation consists simply in the use of the model's general content. One does not pause to scratch one's head over the details.

If we accept for argument's sake that Archilochus is derivative, we must further decide whether he knew these lines from Homer's *Odyssey* (if indeed the text was fixed by Archilochus' time) or some other *Odyssey*. The key phrase is striking, and one likes to feel it is Homer's; but the other possibility cannot be rejected. Conversely, if Homer is derivative the sentiment could have been known to him from lyric poets other than Archilochus. The second alternative may be thought very unlikely, but the first is a real possibility; we must be content to wait for clearer indications that the model in question is a text known to us.

12  Archilochus fr 196

ἀλλά μ' ὁ λυσιμελὴς ὦταῖρε δάμναται πόθος.

Hesiod *Th.* 120ff has been claimed as the model, but the language of both is conventional; compare *Il.* 14.198f, 315f, *Od.* 18.212, Hes. *Th.* 910f, *hVen.* 17, Sappho fr 1.1ff, fr 102.2, fr 130.1, Alcman PMG 3.61, Anacreon PMG 357.1, Carm. Pop. PMG 873.3f..

13  Archilochus fr 201

πόλλ' οἶδ' ἀλώπηξ, ἀλλ' ἐχῖνος ἓν μέγα.

The line recurs in the *Margites* and is called a 'proverb' by the paroemiographers and lexicographers; but it is doubtful that they knew it from any other sources. The reason for this recurrence must remain inscrutable, so that speculation about dependence, or the lack of it, seems fruitless.[65]

14, 15, 16 Archilochus frr 219–21. The three passages are quoted on a papyrus of the third century BC for their imitation of Homer. The first does not provide enough text for one to evaluate the similarity, the third is commonplace; the expression τότε μοι χάνοι εὐρεῖα χθών in the second does not occur outside Homer, but is frequent enough there to support the contention that Archilochus could have heard it in any epic. We have no context to judge what use Archilochus made of it.

17 Archilochus fr 304. Hesychius reports that Archilochus depicted Pyrrhus exulting over the death of Eurypylus; the slaying is mentioned at *Od.* 11.519f. It cannot be shown that Archilochus derived his knowledge of the incident directly from Homer.

The ascription of this fragment is doubted by West. In principle Archilochus (or any Greek poet) can use legendary or mythical material, at least in an exemplum,[66] but it is true that the ascription is not of the sort to inspire confidence. There may be a connection between this fragment and the poem to which fr 134 belonged (οὐ γὰρ ἐσθλὰ κατθανοῦσι κερτομεῖν ἐπ' ἀνδράσιν).

18 The Cologne Epode (S478). Several scholars[67] have thought that the poem is modelled on the Διὸς ἀπάτη in the fourteenth book of the *Iliad*. The general structure is the same in both cases: the man makes his demand; the girl demurs; a compromise is worked out; finally, the act occurs. These scholars have called attention to the bed of flowers on which the consummation takes place in both poems, as well as a verbal parallel between line 3 of Archilochus (εἰ δ' ὧν ἐπείγεαι καί σε θυμὸς ἰθύει) and *Il.* 14.337 (ἀλλ' εἰ δή ῥ' ἐθέλεις καί τοι φίλον ἔπλετο θυμῶι). Moreover, the next line in both cases begins with ἔστιν, and the action of covering with a cloak at the end of Archilochus' poem may recall Zeus and Hera clothing themselves with clouds (line 350, cf 343 ἀμφικαλύψω).

If Archilochus were imitating Homer here, there ought to be more extended verbal similarity (as in frr 131–2 in comparison with *Od.* 18.136f, or Alcaeus fr 347 in comparison with Hes. *Op.* 582ff) to make the point clear to the audience. If, for example, in the lost first portion of the poem, Archilochus had declared that he had never wanted to make love so much as now, and perhaps gone on to enumerate a few other occasions, the relation would be certain. The parallel structure is not sufficient indication in itself, especially since the stages of the seduction are entirely natural. The bed of flowers (later conventional, cf eg *AP* 5.55, Theocr. 5.87) may already have been a common feature of such poems (note Hesiod *Th.* 279).

However, I do concede that the verbal similarities are suggestive if not completely decisive. The allusion, if it does exist, works in a straightforward way; it suggests that 'this experience of mine is like Hera's seduction of Zeus,' no more. It would be a humorous conceit, in keeping with the mock-epic diction employed throughout the poem (see further below p 41). There would be humour too in the abrupt change of tone at line 24; hitherto Archilochus has been solicitous like Zeus, but now he incongruously launches into a dreadful assault on Neoboule.

Such would be the point of the allusion, if it exists. The verbal parallels give only slight support to this belief; it is a slim basis on which to build an interpretation. For if there was nothing else in the lost portion of the fragment which expressed the poet's intention to his audience, then we must suppose that the poem works on two levels, one primary level and another which is unstated and must be inferred by the audience through retrospective analysis. The poet fixes on one particular passage; but instead of incorporating it *in toto* into its new context he merely suggests the model with hints here and there, often at some distance into the poem. The audience may divine the relationship but must then review the first part of the poem mentally and reinterpret it. The examples of imitation so far discussed, and others to be discussed below, do not compel or even invite such an understanding of the methods of early lyric. Rather, the poems take their models and work them into the single, primary level of meaning. The existence of the imitation is signalled at once, and its whole purpose can be grasped as the poem proceeds in oral performance.

If Archilochus is alluding to Homer here, then most readers will accept that he is imitating our *Iliad* or something very like it, since the memorable scene of the fourteenth book is surely Homer's invention. However, it is just possible that the basic idea of the seduction scene antedates Homer, even if the details of the final version are his.

### 19 The Cologne Epode (s478), line 19

π]είσομαι ὥς με κέλεαι.

Others have noted the parallel with *Il.* 23.96 (πείσομαι ὥς σὺ κελεύεις), but Ludwig Koenen has dubbed the line a 'literal quotation.'[68] He goes on to comment:

Achilles agrees to the demand of Patroklos' ghost that they both finally will be buried and reunited in the same urn. Inseparable they will be as they were in life – and so the girl [in Archilochus' poem] is supposed to understand the promise given to her. In the *Iliad*, Achilles' pledge is followed by his futile attempt to embrace Patroklos' ghost.

It is true that the phrase does not occur anywhere else in Homer in exactly this form; but it is simple enough in view of πίθεσθέ μοι ὡς ἀγορεύω (*Od.* 24.461) or ὡς ἂν ἐγὼν εἴπω πειθώμεθα πάντες (eight times in the *Iliad*). At any rate Koenen's conclusion does not seem justified from a simple phrase like 'I will do as you say' expressed in perfectly ordinary Greek (see especially E. Fraenkel, *Beobachtungen zu Aristophanes* [1962] 81ff).

20   Callinus fr 1. T. Krischer has written that this poem is modelled, as others have thought, neither on *Il.* 15.494ff, nor on *Il.* 13.95ff, nor on *Il.* 6.486ff; it is patterned after *Il.* 12.310ff.[69] The similarity between all of these passages is fortuitous and is not very extensive, and the few verbal parallels are hardly compelling. The common sentiments arise naturally from the subject-matter (cf below n 73).

21   Alcman PMG 1.47f ἵππον παγὸν ἀεθλοφόρον καναχάποδα; cf *Il.* 9.123f ἵππους πηγοὺς ἀθλοφόρους; *Certamen* 100, *Ilias Parva* fr xxiii.4 p 136 Allen καναχήποδες ἵπποι. It is unusual for Alcman to use this sort of language; it may be explained by reference to the simile in which it occurs (see below p 40). There is no reason to suppose borrowing directly from *Iliad* 9, as opposed to other epics. What is worth noting is the typically lyric way in which the extra epithet is added (more on this below, p 48).

22   Alcman PMG 77 Δύσπαρις Αἰνόπαρις κακὸν Ἑλλάδι. This is taken to be an imitation of *Il.* 3.39 = 13.769. Although name-play is a widespread poetic device, it is odd that Homer and Alcman should choose the same name; the formation is hardly a common one.[70] On the other hand, there are few characters more likely to be called Δύσ-, and Alcman like Homer may have got the name from tradition. The recurrence of *Il.* 3.39 in a passage widely separated from it (13.769) suggests perhaps that it was embedded in the tradition. The epic βωτιάνειρα occurs because of the heroic context.

23   Alcman PMG 80. Alcman's version of the story is quite different from Homer's. The epithet ταλασίφρων is traditional.

24   Semonides fr 6. Clement (*Strom.* 6.13.1) compares this fragment with Hes. *Op.* 702f. The idea is not difficult, especially for the poet of fr 7, and ῥίγιον is not an unlikely adjective in the context; but the particular verb ληΐζεται may be thought to confirm that Semonides is borrowing. As in previous cases the thought is simply taken over wholesale by the imitator.

25   Semonides fr 7.110f, fr 1. Hermann Fränkel, *Dichtung und Philosophie* 235, thinks that fr 7.110f imitates Hesiod *Op.* 701; but the idea that a bad wife will cause one's neighbours to laugh at one is commonplace, as the Cologne Archilochus (s478.33f) shows. Because of this parallel and the one in fr 6, Fränkel argues (235 n 8) that parallels between Semonides fr 1 and Hesiod's *Works and Days* must also be examples of direct borrowing, though in themselves they do not compel that assumption. He cites (231 n 2)

lines 1–2 ~ 669; 1–3 ~ 105; 11–12 ~ 92–3; 15–17 ~ 686–7; 20 ~ 100–1; 23 ~ 58. Fränkel is aware that these are mostly commonplaces; the parallel of lines 15–17 ~ 686–7 may be more precise, but it is uncertain that Semonides' εὖτ' ἄν μὴ δυνήσωνται ζόειν refers to poverty. In any event, the argument that one imitation guarantees another is fallacious. Certainly Semonides knew his Hesiod, but the idea of an archaic poet borrowing bits and pieces from here and there to make his poem is implausible.

26 Tyrtaeus fr 10.21ff. The many arguments advanced in the discussion of these lines in comparison with *Il.* 22.71–6 will not usefully be repeated here. I accept that the passages are connected because of the occurrence in each of two specific details: the genitals of the old man, and the sentiment 'all things are seemly for youth.'[71] There is however no conclusive force in any argument for the priority of either passage.[72] The change in emphasis is very easy: in Homer, it is that an old man's violent death is piteous; in Tyrtaeus, that his death in battle is disgraceful.

27 Tyrtaeus fr 11.29–34: see above, p 24. Homer describes close fighting; Tyrtaeus exhorts men to engage in it. If Tyrtaeus is actually copying Homer here, then the imitation extends to little more than the addition of more parts of armour to the list.

28 Tyrtaeus fr 11.11–14

οἳ μὲν γὰρ τολμῶσι παρ' ἀλλήλοισι μένοντες
ἔς τ' αὐτοσχεδίην καὶ προμάχους ἰέναι,
παυρότεροι θνήσκουσι, σαοῦσι δὲ λαὸν ὀπίσσω·
τρεσσάντων δ' ἀνδρῶν πᾶσ' ἀπόλωλ' ἀρετή.

Compare *Il.* 5.529–32 (~15.561–4):

ὦ φίλοι, ἀνέρες ἔστε καὶ ἄλκιμον ἦτορ ἔλεσθε,
ἀλλήλους τ' αἰδεῖσθε κατὰ κρατερὰς ὑσμίνας·
αἰδομένων ἀνδρῶν πλέονες σόοι ἠὲ πέφανται·
φευγόντων δ' οὔτ' ἄρ κλέος ὄρνυται οὔτε τις ἀλκή.

The content of the first two lines in each passage is similar; the subject of both is the soldier in his relation to others in the front lines. The similarity in the content and (antithetical) structure of the last two lines is more obvious. No verbal parallel exists unless σαοῦσι ~ σόοι is counted.

Owing to the nature of Tyrtaeus' subject, there are bound to be thematic connections with Homer and other epic poetry,[73] and it could be argued that the parallels are fortuitous. It seems likely, however, that the memory of the Homeric passage was at the back of Tyrtaeus' mind. Yet that is all that need be said to explain the similarities. There is no indication in the form of significant changes of detail that Tyrtaeus worked through his model a word at a time, adopting, rejecting, or modifying as he went.

Those who use the fragments of Tyrtaeus as evidence for *Geistesgeschichte*, however, assume that the poet followed just such a procedure. In an influential piece, Werner Jaeger argued that Tyrtaeus re-fashioned Homer's notion of ἀρετή in accordance with Spartan social ideals.[74] Others have followed Jaeger both in their technique of analysis and in finding a new ἀρετή in Tyrtaeus, and although they may differ considerably in their results, these works are really of a kind.[75] As an aside, it is surprising that none of the principal adherents of this school has tried to claim that certain small-scale changes in the passage under discussion are significant. Tyrtaeus' men are encouraged to 'endure' (line 11; cf above n 52); σαοῦσι δὲ λαὸν ὀπίσσω (13) could be a reference to the Spartan battle formation, and, in keeping with the poet's social values, to the individual's responsibility to his peers; ἀρετή (14) has replaced Homer's ἀλκή, and his ideal of κλέος has been omitted.[76] But the whole thesis that Tyrtaeus has somehow changed the meaning of the word ἀρετή is wrong, as Campbell rightly protests.[77] The verses on which this view is apparently based, ἥδ᾽ ἀρετή, τόδ᾽ ἄεθλον ἐν ἀνθρώποισιν / κάλλιστόν τε φέρειν γίνεται ἀνδρὶ νέωι (fr 12.13–14), are better translated as 'this ἀρετή, this prize is best to win ... ' than as 'this is ἀρετή, this is the best prize for a young man to win.'[78] There are other ἀρεταί. In fr 12.2, Tyrtaeus speaks of the ἀρετή of foot-racing; the other skills mentioned in the first lines of that poem are by implication ἀρεταί as well (cf also fr 12.43). In line 14 of the poem here discussed, he says rather ingenuously, 'Once men fear, all courage is lost.' The word ἀρετή here has no more 'moral,' 'inner' or 'social' significance than it does in Homer or in other early authors. When Socrates asks, 'What is the ἀρετή of the *soul?*', the very form of the question marks a revolution in perception, and reveals that the word had changed little until that time.

29   Mimnermus fr 2.1ff (late seventh century). Many have taken this passage to be an elaboration of *Il.* 6.146ff. The central thought may be a commonplace, but in this case one suspects that it is Homer who has made the thought famous, and thenceforward a commonplace. The simile is striking, and likely to be the invention of a poet. 'Simonides,' fr 8 West, actually quotes the Homeric line;[79] compare further Bacchyl. 5.65, Ar. *Av.* 685, Ap. Rhod. 4.216f, Verg. *Aen.* 6.309f.

Homer's concern is the succession of generations that renders a particular generation and a man's life insignificant. In Mimnermus the emphasis is on the brevity of youth, and on the evils which befall men when it is gone. Comparison with Semonides fr 1 and 'Simonides' fr 8 West shows that we are dealing again with a group of traditional ideas;[80] different ideas in this group are important to different poets, so that they state them in various orders and with varying emphases. Mimnermus is not correcting Homer; indeed his own point is clear without reference to Homer's text.[81]

To pause and review these seventh-century passages: although subjective judgment is unavoidable in many cases, it is clear that many more passages have been claimed as imitations of epic than can be proved. Those imitations we have accepted as probable or certain generally reveal the same relationship to their models: in Archilochus frr 131–2, Tyrtaeus frr 10.21ff and 11.11–14, Semonides fr 6 and Mimnermus fr 2, the main idea has been taken over completely; details are then added or an emphasis changed as the immediate context demands. A similar analysis obtains in Tyrtaeus fr 11.29–34, if that is indeed a case of borrowing.

The question is whether in any of these passages we really need to recall the details of the model in order to understand the point of the imitation. The passages in Archilochus and Semonides provide no context to help us decide. The Tyrtaean passage would presumably be recognized by the audience as Homeric. The poet's purpose is to evoke in a general way the heroic atmosphere of Homer in order to inspire his fellow Spartans. That is easy enough, and not quite the same thing as requiring the reader to ponder the original context and to discover which aspects of the model are relevant. In Tyrtaeus fr 10.21ff the poet may intend us to recall the intense emotion of the original context and transfer some of it to the new context, but we cannot be sure; if this is so, the poem resembles the type of two-level composition just described. The Cologne epode of Archilochus may come even closer, but that is problematic (see above).

All of these passages may be imitations of a fixed text of Homer (except Semonides, who of course imitates the fixed text of Hesiod). We cannot, however, be certain that Homer's text was fixed at this time; for certainty, we must wait for Alcaeus, Stesichorus, and Ibycus (see below). The point is important. As the idea of a fixed, written text takes hold, imitation becomes more precise. In the seventh century culture was still predominantly oral, and it is no surprise that Homer's text had not yet ousted all the others (if indeed Homer's text existed then; but most now accept this). The whole epic corpus continued to form the background of numerous poems; these poems have an epic cast but no specific Homeric reference.

### Sixth Century

1 Hipponax frr 72, 74–7. There is no indication that Hipponax derived his knowledge of the Rhesus episode in fr 72 directly from Homer, though it

is probable that he did. In frr 74–7 there seem to be references to Odyssean stories, but it is impossible to tell what the source or context was.

2  Theognis 239f θοίνηις δὲ καὶ εἰλαπίνηισι παρέσσηι / ἐν πάσαις. Compare *Il.* 10.217 ἀεὶ δ' ἐν δαίτηισι καὶ εἰλαπίνηισι παρέσται. The expression θοίνηις ... καὶ εἰλαπίνηισι has the pleonastic aspect of epic language, so Theognis is probably looking in that direction; there is no guarantee, however, of a connection with this particular Homeric passage, since a man's presence at feasts is a customary mark of honour everywhere in epic. Theognis uses 'presence' in a different way; the boy will not be physically present, but rather present as the subject of banqueters' songs. Some critics have thought that this difference results from modifying a Homeric model, but it is merely a natural part of Theognis' central conceit, 'my songs have given you wings to fly about the world, and you will be famous.' His own song, one presumes, is sung at a symposium; when he thinks of the spreading of the boy's fame, he naturally thinks of similar settings elsewhere. The metaphor of the song's wings is the heart of the poem, and has no parallel in epic.

3  Solon frr 4 and 11. Werner Jaeger argued that the two passages show knowledge of *Od.* 1.32ff, where Zeus denies that the gods are responsible for men's woes.[82] Solon says in fr 4 that the citizens' folly and greed will destroy the city; in fr 11 he says expressly that the Athenians must not blame the gods for their troubles. For verbal parallels, Jaeger offers αὐτοί in 4.5 and 11.3 ~ αὐτοί in *Od.* 1.33, and ἀφραδίηισιν in 4.5 ~ σφῆισιν ἀτασθαλίηισιν in *Od.* 1.34. Both, however, arise naturally from the point being made, and in the absence of more extensive parallels we must look for other evidence to decide the question of borrowing. One small detail, which, I believe, has gone unnoticed, suggests that Solon is independent. The opening lines do not describe a situation in any way similar to that of the divine council in the *Odyssey*. There Zeus disclaims all responsibility for the troubles men bring on themselves. Solon says 'Our city will never be destroyed by decree of Zeus and the other gods, for Athena is our protector.' This might actually imply that were it not for Athena the gods would indeed punish the city; however, we are probably meant not to think of Athena holding a furious pack of Olympians at bay, but rather of a heaven united by her persuasion. Still, the point is that whatever happens in heaven, we are not to worry about it; let Athena do that. We must acknowledge our responsibility and set about solving our problems. The question of the gods' responsibility or lack of it is simply used as foil for the main subject. The poem is not a theodicy.[83] Here, as in all his poems, Solon is speaking as a man of action who needs to find practical solutions to difficult political problems. He sees the greed and factionalism of his fellow citizens and urges them here,

as in his elegy to the Muses, to realize that the current state of affairs is their own doing and can be set right. Jaeger, of course, was mainly concerned to show that the conception of δίκη in Solon is different from that of Homer and Hesiod; whether he is right on this score is another question. As far as the influence of *Odyssey* 1 is concerned, Jaeger's incorrect belief that the poem was a theodicy led him to think that it imitated Homer. There are no extensive verbal parallels, and we have seen that Solon's opening lines make a rather different point from Homer's. As for the general idea that men can bring evil on themselves, we may suspect that Solon did not need Homer and Hesiod to teach him that.

4  Solon fr 13.21–2 θεῶν ἕδος αἰπὺν ἱκάνει / οὐρανόν, αἰθρίην δ' αὖτις ἔθηκεν ἰδεῖν. Compare *Il.* 5.360, 367, 868; 8.456; 17.646; *hAp.* 109. Solon is aiming for an elevated tone in his simile, and he borrows extensively from epic – in general; there is nothing to indicate dependence on a particular passage.[84]

5  Solon fr 13.29–32. The passage is parallel to *Il.* 4.160–2; it is also parallel to Theognis 203ff, Hdt. 6.86 γ 2, Aesch. *Ag.* 750–1. The sentiment is conventional wisdom.

6  Solon fr 13.55f τὰ δὲ μόρσιμα πάντως / οὔτε τις οἰωνὸς ῥύσεται οὔθ' ἱερά: cf *Il.* 2.859 ἀλλ' οὐκ οἰωνοῖσιν ἐρύσατο κῆρα μέλαιναν. The general form of the statement in Solon suggests a gnomic background, but without further evidence from the archaic period this possibility cannot be affirmed.

7  Solon fr 36.27. The simile of a wolf whirling about in the midst of a pack of dogs is close to that in *Il.* 12.41f (κάπριος ἠὲ λέων). This passage may indeed be Solon's model; but similes involving animals at bay are frequent in epic, and there is nothing against Solon's free invention of this one, independently of his recall of specific passages.

8  Stesichorus *PMG* 209. This fragment is clearly inspired by Homer, *Od.* 15.16off. The incident described is of a particular nature; it is unlikely to have been a traditional part of every Odyssey. Moreover, the omen has been inserted in Homer's *Odyssey* in order to create anticipation; it is part of a structure which goes all the way back to Book 1.

Not enought of the text survives for us to determine what use Stesichorus made of this episode, and whether any changes of detail are significant. There is a mysterious crow at i 9; the statement οὐδ' ἐγώ σ' ἐρύξω (i 10) is given to Menelaus in Homer, to Helen here (whose speech – if she is still the speaker, as seems likely – is longer in Stesichorus).

9  Stesichorus s15 ii 15ff. Images of injured or weighed-down flowers in similes were not unusual (Sappho fr 105b), but the comparison to a dying man's head may be particular enough to suggest a borrowing from *Il.*

8.306ff. Whether the details varied is not clear from the text of Stesichorus; he may have gone on to say, like Homer, that the poppy swayed from the weight of its fruit and the rain. But it is of little import whether he did or did not. A noticeable difference is the statement of Stesichorus that the poppy, in its failing and loss of leaves, violates its usual beauty. The ugliness of Geryon's death is thus emphasized. Not for Homer such direct and explicit appeals, nor the use of loaded words like καταισχύνοισα. His simile is no less evocative and pathetic; but he says only 'the poppy swayed its head from side to side.' The difference between the poets is considerable, but does not arise from subtle rewriting on Stesichorus' part; it arises from the different concerns of the two genres. Subtlety is illustrated rather by what the Latin poets do with the image (Catullus 11.21ff, cf 62.39ff; Verg. Aen. 9.435ff): the flower is variously plucked and forgotten, injured by a passing plough, stands in the farthest field, or is nicked in the stem and left to die slowly. This sentimental note is not in Stesichorus' text as it stands, and I doubt that it would be if we had more of it.[85]

10   Stesichorus s11. Compare Il. 12.322ff. It is part of Homer's 'heroic creed', and a recurrent theme in Greek literature, that because men are mortal they must earn a substitute immortality through their achievements; they must live aggressively, and strive for glory while they can. Sarpedon's statement of this view, however, is a significant event in the Iliad, and the form it takes is remarkable for its nearly paradoxical quality: because we are mortal, he says, we must risk our lives in battle. One would expect the conclusion to be exactly the opposite. It is very likely that Stesichorus has this passage in mind here; the same notable reasoning is stated at length. There seems to be no real difference in the treatment; Stesichorus' is no more or less pathetic than Homer's. As in other passages, only a general recollection of Homer's text need be supposed here; the one close verbal parallel (lines 8f ∼ 323) does not require us to believe that Stesichorus had the exact text of Homer in mind.

11   Ibycus PMG 282(a) (s151). J.P. Barron suggests that lines 23ff are an allusion to Iliad 2.484–93, the invocation before the Catalogue of the Ships.[86] Two motifs are common: the knowledge of the Muses and the ignorance of men, and the seemingly endless burden of narration that is beyond the teller's capacity. Both these points can easily be paralleled elsewhere; that they are combined with a reference to the ships at Aulis (27ff) in a poem reciting the main figures of the Trojan war, however, makes the connection between the two passages very likely.

Few will doubt that by this date Ibycus refers to a fixed text of Homer essentially the same as ours. This poem is the first certain example we have encountered where the passage imitated must be recalled by the audience in order to understand the point of the imitation; the mind's eye has to look two places at once, and the listener is left to make all necessary inferences. The inferences, however, are quickly made. We realize that not only is the subject of the song associated with heroic themes, but the singer is likened to the most famous epic poet and his poem (cf ὡς κατ' ἀοιδὰν καὶ ἐμὸν κλέος in the last line). To discover this we do not need to sit down with the two written texts and compare them in detail.

Barron also thinks that Hesiod Op. 646–62 may lie behind the Ibycean passage because the words σεσοφισμένος, Ἑλικώνιδες, πολύγομφος and Αὐλίς occur in both. The point presumably would be that Ibycus compares his own effort also to Hesiod's prize-winning achievement. Yet two sophisticated allusions in the same passage should perhaps give us pause, especially since the second depends on single words and not a similarity of context. However, one of these words (πολύγομφος) does not occur elsewhere in the archaic period, and σεσοφισμέναι is strikingly applied to the Muses. These facts perhaps make imitation likely; if that is indeed the case the poem represents a dramatic departure from the norm and bespeaks a growing precision and sophistication in the art of lyric composition.

12    Alcaeus fr 44. This is an allusion to an event of central importance in the *Iliad*, Thetis' supplication of Zeus. The reason for her visit and its consequences are assumed to be common knowledge. Since the poet alludes in a few words to the whole of the *Iliad*, and since few will believe that another full-length *Iliad* (or even a 'Wrath-poem') existed alongside Homer's ca 600 BC, this passage refers to the poem as we know it.

The example of the Cologne Alcaeus (fr 298 = S262) allows us to believe that the story was being used as a mythological exemplum: Alcaeus' opponents will be crushed as surely as the Trojans, and his party vindicated as surely as Achilles. The inference is clear and easy, but it is an inference, so that the poem perhaps works like the poem by Ibycus above. In the latter case, of course, there were two discrete allusions, whereas Alcaeus has only one; that Alcaeus' poem is at least half a century earlier perhaps makes it easier to believe that Ibycus could employ such a technique.

13    Alcaeus fr 347.[87] Compare Hes. Op. 582ff. The fragment is undoubtedly an imitation; the extended verbal coincidence and the particularity of the details are too pronounced for it to be otherwise. Some points made by Hesiod are not found in Alcaeus' poem, but then only part of it is extant. Certainly there is no discernible reason for the selection of those details we do have, and the omission of others; nor is there any profound reason for the substitution of μιαρώτατοι and λέπτοι for Hesiod's μαχλότατοι and ἀφαυρότατοι.[88] Alcaeus has organized the argument more effectively, however, by placing τέγγε πλεύμονας οἴνωι at the beginning, as

a 'heading' or general statement of the poem's content and purpose, followed by supporting details, as often in archaic lyric.[89] We cannot be certain that Alcaeus went on to make something new of this material, but it is perhaps likely that he did not. This is a drinking song, probably a short exhortation on the subject; after completing his 'transition' Alcaeus may have repeated the injunction of the opening line to round things off. It seems that Alcaeus simply took Hesiod over *in toto*, varying the details only insignificantly and organizing the poem in a slightly different way to suit his own taste and immediate requirements.

14    Sappho fr 1. J. Svenbro has made an elaborate case that this poem is modelled on the passage of the *Iliad* where Athena descends from Olympus to help Diomedes.[90] Athena's preparations are described at *Il.* 5.733ff:

Αὐτὰρ Ἀθηναίη, κούρη Διὸς αἰγιόχοιο,
πέπλον μὲν κατέχευεν ἑανὸν πατρὸς ἐπ' οὔδει,
ποικίλον, ὅν ῥ' αὐτὴ ποιήσατο καὶ κάμε χερσίν·
ἡ δὲ χιτῶν' ἐνδῦσα Διὸς νεφεληγερέταο
τεύχεσιν ἐς πόλεμον θωρήσσετο δακρυόεντα ...
ἐς δ' ὄχεα φλόγεα ποσὶ βήσετο, λάζετο δ' ἔγχος
βριθὺ μέγα στιβαρόν, τῶι δάμνησι στίχας ἀνδρῶν
ἡρώων, οἷσίν τε κοτέσσεται ὀβριμοπάτρη.
Ἥρη δὲ μάστιγι θοῶς ἐπεμαίετ' ἄρ' ἵππους·
αὐτόμαται δὲ πύλαι μύκον οὐρανοῦ, ἃς ἔχον Ὧραι,
τῆις ἐπιτέτραπται μέγας οὐρανὸς Οὔλυμπός τε,
ἠμὲν ἀνακλῖναι πυκινὸν νέφος ἠδ' ἐπιθεῖναι.

Svenbro finds six points of contact: (1) Athena is called 'daughter of Zeus' as Aphrodite is called 'child of Zeus'; (2) Athena has a πέπλος ποικίλος, and Aphrodite is ποικιλόθρονος (derived, I believe correctly, from θρόνα);[91] (3) Athena goes ἐς πόλεμον, and Aphrodite is called a σύμμαχος; (4) the verb δαμνάω is used of both goddesses; (5) Athena's chariot is drawn by ἵπποι, while Aphrodite's is drawn by στροῦθοι; (6) as Athena departs, the gates of heaven open, whereas Aphrodite is said to leave her father's house. Furthermore, in lines 729ff the yoking of the horses to a golden chariot is described, offering a parallel to lines 8–9 of Sappho's poem (taking χρύσιον with ἄρμα); and in lines 767ff the flight of the chariot 'between earth and starry heaven' is parallel to ἀπ' ὠράνω αἴθερος διὰ μέσσω in Sappho.

It is hard to see wherein (5) and (6) consist, since the chariots must be drawn by something, and must leave from somewhere. (1) is a conventional form of address for Aphrodite; in (2) it is not pointed out that Athena is here discarding her fancy garb. As for the rest, one might just as well claim that

*Iliad* 13.10ff is the model: Poseidon descends from a height to prevent the rout of the Greeks (note δαμναμένους, 16); he goes off to a golden palace (21f, significant if one takes χρύσιον with δόμον in Sappho, but this apart there is still plenty of gold in the passage, in Poseidon's clothes – cf ποικιλόθρονος? -, his whip and his horses' manes); his horses are swift (31) like Sappho's sparrows; and he moves amid general delight (cf Sappho's μειδιαίσαισα) of the natural world ἐς ᾿Αχαιῶν νῆας (cf σύμμαχος)! Neither passage is a model for Sappho. Indeed, the indications Sappho gives to her audience are so weak and indecisive that the poem must be termed a failure. Yet it is not; the details of her description have full meaning within their own context. Sappho's poem is not a cryptic re-evaluation of the heroic world nor, as Svenbro has it, a desperate clinging to that world in a time of rapid change.

Our survey is now complete. The general picture that emerges for the sixth century is the same as for the seventh. However, there are more certain or near-certain imitations of Homer's poetry in the form in which we know it, and a few examples in which poets require the audience to make its own inferences about the relation of copy to model. Yet no poet uses a technique of imitation that depends on subtle changes in individual words; there are no Virgils here.

EPIC DICTION IN LYRIC POETRY

Turning now to examine the use of epic diction in the lyric poets, I can refer the reader to Harvey's excellent study and to the various works cited above (n 47), and dispense with long lists of parallels here. Most readers, if they work through the poets, will know for themselves what is epic; I shall rely on this knowledge and select only the important examples for discussion. I am concerned to discover the poetic uses of epic language. It was a necessary step to compare the use of a phrase in a lyric poem and in Homer; but this is only half the exercise. As I have argued above, 'Homer' has been too easily equated with 'the epic.' Let us consider these phrases simply as epic, and get on with seeing how they operate in their own contexts.

This study bears out and supplements Harvey's conclusions, which may be summarized here. He found that epicisms fall easily into several categories: (1) heroic contexts; (2) hymnodic contexts; (3) mention of divinities; (4) nature (principally earth and sea). A fifth category includes words found but not especially frequent in epic, which have become favourite words in the lyric poets' vocabulary (eg ἁβρός, ἁπαλός, ἐρατός, ἀγλαός). I would add place-names (including with them the word πόλις), and make a special category for the word 'ship,' which is usually given an epithet in lyric; and I would observe that in similes the amount of epic vocabulary increases noticeably. A good example is Solon fr 13.18ff.[92] Harvey concluded that, because the use of epic epithets is fairly predictable, lyric poets do not use them indiscriminately. Their intention is to create the effect of epic language by employing it in a few contexts where epicisms are particularly at home. The use of such language is a matter of choice; poets are not slaves to it.

Two further observations made by Harvey need to be reported. He noted the way in which lyric poets often combine genuine and pseudo-epic epithets, or a genuine epithet with a favourite lyric word. This tendency supports the conclusion that their use of epic diction is conscious and deliberate. Secondly, Harvey found several examples of what he designated 'mock-heroic' use of the epic language. The trick of using epicisms to achieve humour through incongruity or the tone of swagger they engender is important in the iambographers; further comments will be made below.

Harvey may be criticized, however, for his use of the word 'clichés' to describe epic formulae; it imports misleading connotations. It would be more correct to say that a certain manner of speaking was recognized as high style, and that it could be judiciously employed without impugning what we should call 'originality.' Plainly there was no objection to any poet saying 'black earth,' as we might object to someone who says 'eyes of limpid blue.' This was an age accustomed to formulaic oral poetry, in which craftsmanship worked on the level of the phrase rather than individual words. The desire for the *mot juste* belongs to a later age. The change of emphasis from formulae to words can be discerned in the technique of the lyric poets; it is a stylistic development encouraged by the shorter compass of their compositions. By the time we reach Anacreon, there is a great deal of attention paid to each word in the poem (yet even he can say πορφύρεα κύματα, PMG 347.18). Indeed, there is an apparent contradiction here between the way in which epic content is usually transferred *en bloc* from model to copy, and the conscious and careful applications often made of particular phrases taken from the epic language. But the contradiction readily resolves itself when one reflects upon the nature of lyric in the period; the poetry is very much on the surface, in the clear and straightforward formulation of ideas, in the ornaments and style, not beneath the surface in the subtleties of poet-reader relations, remote literary resonances, etc.

Archilochus illustrates these claims particularly well. On the one hand he uses a judicious amount of epic phrasing and vocabulary to elevate the tone of his poems. Such is clearly the case in frr 8, 9, 12, and 13, where the contexts are serious. Since we have no context in frr 4 and 5, their tone is impossible to estimate; fr 4 is an invitation to get drunk on duty, and may be riotous, while fr 5 could be delivered in a tone of bluff and false bravado. The epicisms would on this view be called 'mock-epic.' The poems may, conversely, be quite serious, so that the epicisms add elevation. Fr 2 has no real Homericism in it; fr 1 is a good illustration of the force and sharpness Archilochus can achieve while using highly traditional language. The use of the high style in serious contexts is illustrated further by frr 128, 130 and 131.

On the other hand Archilochus uses his language precisely. Few of his epic adjectives are unnecessary (fr 4.6 θοῆς ... νηός; fr 4.8 οἶνον ἐρυθρόν). δεσπόται Εὐβοίης δουρικλυτοί in fr 3.5 is surprising, since the poet has just been making much of the Euboeans' ability with the sword; Page proposed ἄορι κλυτοί. I had been inclined to accept this, but rejected it on considering[93] that the thrusting of spears is another example, like swords, of fighting at close quarters; such fighting, in contrast to long-range archery and slinging, is the central point, as Plutarch notes. Hence the adjective is, again, precisely used. Others make quite pointed sense: ἔντος ἀμώμητον in fr 5.2 ('and a very good shield it was, too'); καθαρός in fr 9.11 makes the picture vivid. The same close attention to diction can be observed in the colourful verbs in fr 4, ἄφελκε and ἄγρει; in γυναικεῖον πένθος, fr 13.10; οἴνωι συγκεραυνωθεὶς φρένας, fr 120.2; ὑπὸ καρδίην ἐλυσθείς, fr 191.1; ἄψυχος, fr 193.2. In fr 6, ξείνια δυσμενέσιν λυγρὰ χαριζόμενοι is a deliberate (double) oxymoron.

The same care with detail is reflected in the elegant structure which the poems often exhibit (a trait Archilochus shares with Anacreon). Fr 1 speaks for itself; fr 2 has its triple ἐν δορί. Fr 13 shows what Fränkel called a 'gradual pointing of thought and sharpening of tone,'[94] to conclude with ἀλλὰ τάχιστα τλῆτε, γυναικεῖον πένθος ἀπωσάμενοι. Fr 128 is similar: γίνωσκε δ᾽ οἷος ῥυσμὸς ἀνθρώπους ἔχει brings the fragment to a sharp close. There is a rhythm to fr 105 produced by the varying length of the cola and the placing of the words πόντος, νέφος, and φόβος. Fr 114 breaks down into two couplets, the first a smooth and balanced composition, the second choppy and forceful, leading up to καρδίης πλέως by means of cola decreasing in length. Frr 120 and 176 resemble one another in the way they keep a sharp point until the end of the sense-unit, and express it in an appended participial phrase.[95]

Examples of mock-epic in Archilochus are not lacking, though sometimes one has to accept a particular interpretation of a fragment in order to see them. Frr 191 and 193 are possible instances, if the irony is not bitter but humorous. Mock-epic is understandable if a humorous or sexual interpretation is appropriate. In the Cologne Epode (s478), there are several examples: καί σε θυμὸς ἰθύει, line 3; εἶδος ἄμωμον, line 7; possibly the matronymic in line 10; the epithets for Amphimedo in line 11; ἣν νῦν γῆ κατ' εὑρώεσσ' ἔχει, line 12; ἐς ποη[φόρους / κ]ήπους, line 23f.⁹⁶ πέτρης ἐπὶ προβλῆτος, fr 41.2; ποῖον ἐφράσω τόδε; τίς σὰς παρήειρε φρένας / ἧις τὸ πρὶν ἠρήρησθα; fr 172.1ff should also be noted.⁹⁷

The use of compound adjectives with proper names in invective, too, has affinities with mock-epic. Such adjectives often resemble epic ones, and sometimes one can see that the poet has coined them with precisely an epic effect in mind. When Hipponax (fr 128) says Μοῦσά μοι Εὐρυμεδοντιάδεα τὴν ποντοχάρυβδιν, / τὴν ἐγγαστριμάχαιραν ... ἔννεπε, mock-epic intent is obvious from the parody of invocation form. Archilochus fr 117 τὸν κεροπλάστην ἄειδε Γλαῦκον is similar. Hipponax fr 12.2 has ὁ μητροκοίτης Βούπαλος; fr 28.1 Μιμνῆ κατωμόχανε. We may add the names Alcaeus invented for Pittacus (fr 429); perhaps Alcman PMG 17.4 ὁ παμφάγος Ἀλκμάν (a joke at his own expense, not unknown in Alcman); Asius fr 14 (West, Iambi et Elegi II 46); Anacreon PMG 346.13 λεωφόρ' Ἡροτίμη, PMG 349.1f. Ἰηλυσίους ... κυανάσπιδας, PMG 372.2 ὁ περιφόρητος Ἀρτέμων, perhaps PMG 387 τὸν μυροποιὸν ... Στράττιν, PMG 433 Ἐρξίωνι / τῶι λευκολόφωι, PMG 427.2f τῆι πολυκρότηι ... Γαστροδώρηι.⁹⁸ PMG 394(b) φαλακρὸς Ἄλεξις may be in the same spirit, although the adjective is not an epic compound. The invective in these examples varies in intensity; in Anacreon, some of them are party-jokes, friendly teasing of his fellow symposiasts.⁹⁹

Epic diction in Hipponax is rare except when used for mock-epic effect. Deities usually retain their epithets in lyric; in fr 3a, a parody of the hymn-form (as are frr 32 and 38; cf fr 35), the epithets are humorous. πολύστονος in fr 39.1 makes good sense, and may well be mock-epic. In fr 128 (see above) the endings of lines 2, 3 and 4 are all traditional; ὅπως in line 3 and πῶς in fr 129 are probably correctly retained as part of the parody (West, Studies 90).

Apart from fr 72, where the epicisms are explained by the context, there is no straightforward use of the epic such as we find in fr 115 (the Strasbourg epode) line 4 κύμ[ατι] πλα[ζόμ]ενος (Od 5.388f) and line 6 Θρήϊκες ἀκρό[κ]ομοι (Il. 4.533).¹⁰⁰ This is not an argument in itself for Archilochean authorship, though it may provide some support for that view. The invective here, though losing nothing in force and probably gaining by it, has no vulgar or colloquial element. The piece is reminiscent of Alcaeus in more ways than one.

In the collection of poems bearing the name of Theognis we find much that is of interest. Many of the pieces were composed for the symposium by amateurs who turned to the epic for the occasional elevated phrase. Often they would use a well established formula, just as they found it; at other times they would introduce small modifications. Many of the epithets in the *Theognidea* are not attested in extant epic, but are plainly inspired by it; among them is the occasional ἅπαξ λεγόμενον (eg πολυκώκυτος 244). In the amateurish pieces, there are fewer epicisms than in a poet such as Archilochus, but there are more purely ornamental epithets. In those poems of the corpus which come from a superior hand, we find a more extended and precise use of the epic; the longer pieces 237–54, 699–718 and 773–88 are artistic efforts, and give a strong Homeric impression.

The poetic abilities of inscription-writers are comparable for the most part to those of the Theognidean authors. The parallel is not uninstructive. A glance through Hansen's *Carmina Epigraphica Graeca* reveals a very similar technique in the use of epicism. The authors lend dignity to their efforts by employing an epic phrase or two, often formulae with little or no alteration. Note for example πένθος ἄλαστον (Hansen no 59); βαρέα στενάχοντες (139.2); κλέϝος ἄφθιτον αἰϝεί (344.2); (ἐπ)εύχεται εἶναι (195.2); κατὰ γαῖ᾽ ἐκάλυψεν (76.1). Epic language is nearly inevitable in descriptions of deities (Ποτειδάωνι ϝάνακτι, Διὸς γλαυ⟨κ⟩ώπιδι ⟨κ⟩ούρηι, ϝεκαβόλωι Ἀπόλλωνι, etc). The author of no 40.2 has lifted half a line from Homer (τὸ γὰρ γέρας ἐστὶ θανόντων, *Il.* 16.457); in nos 6, 82, 145 and 155 we find the Homeric verb μάρνασθαι written with a β according to local pronunciation.[101]

An interesting phenomenon found both in the *Theognidea* and in verse-inscriptions may be termed 'pseudo-formulae.' The pressures of the metre and the recurrence of a subject on different occasions lead to the repeated use of the same words in the same position. There are many examples of this verbal patterning, and they have been examined in detail by P. Giannini.[102] Some recurrences may be accidental, like the tendency of comparatives, superlatives, and middle/passive participles to occupy the end of the pentameter. γίνεται is found after the diaeresis of the pentameter 34 times in elegy. χαλεπώτατον ἄχθος in Theognis 295 recurs in the same position at 1384; similarly lines 386 ~ 630, 474 ~ 722 (= Sol. fr 24.4), 920 ~ 1000; 81 ~ *IG* I³ 722.2 (*IG* I² 471, Hansen no 225). Other parallels are more significant; note for example the following groups:

1  74 πιστὸν ἔχουσι νόον (so 698)
    580 κοῦφον ἔχοντα νόον
    498 κοῦφον ἔθηκε νόον (cf 196 τλήμονα θῆκε
                        νόον, same position)
    88 = 1082d πιστὸς ἔνεστι νόος
    622 αὐτὸς ἔνεστι νόος
    792 ἐσθλὸν ἔχοιμι νόον

Sol. fr 11.6 χαῦνος ἔνεστι νόος
814, 1016 ὅντιν' ἔχουσι νόον
312 (~214, 1072) ἥντιν' ἕκαστος ἔχει
898 νοῦν ἕκαστος ἔχει (cf Euenus fr 3.2
        (ὀρθῶς γινώσκειν)
        οἷος ἕκαστος ἀνήρ,
        same position; Il. 22.382
        ὄφρα κ' ἔτι
        γνῶμεν Τρώων νόον ὅντιν'
        ἔχουσιν)

367 has νόον ἀστῶν ὅντιν' ἔχουσιν at the end of a hexameter; its doublet
1184a has γνῶναι νόον ὅντιν' ἔχουσιν (cf Il. 22.382). Compare also
Archilochus fr 185.6 πυκνὸν ἔχουσα νόον.

**2**  340 μοῖρα κίχηι θανάτου
    820 μοῖρα λάβοι θανάτου
    Callin. fr 1.15 μοῖρα κίχεν θανάτου
    Simon. fr 119.2 Bergk μοῖρ' ἔκιχεν θανάτου
    Mimn. fr 6.2 = Sol. fr 20.0; Sol. fr 20.4 μοῖρα κίχοι
                                   θανάτου
    Sol. fr 13.30 μοῖρ' ἐπιοῦσα κίχηι
    Sol. fr 27.18 μοῖραν ἔχοι θανάτου
    Tyrt. fr 7.2 μοῖρα κίχοι θανάτου

Epic has μοῖρα ... θανάτοιο four times in the Odyssey, once in the Iliad, once
in the Hymns and once in Hesiod; but most often θάνατος καὶ μοῖρα is
used. For the verb κιχεῖν cf eg Il. 17.478 = 672 = 22.436; IG XII 9.286
(Eretria, VI BC; Hansen no 77) θανάτου δὲ ἐνθάδε μοῖρ' ἔχιχε and IG XII
8.397 (Thasos, ca 500; Hansen no 158) μοῖρα κίχηι θανάτου, at the end of
the pentameter, as in the examples above.

**3**  422 πόλλ' ἀμέλητα πέλει
    984 ἔργ' ἐρατεινὰ φέρηι
    1290 ἔργ' ἀτέλεστα τέλει
    Simon. fr 8.7 West πόλλ' ἀτέλεστα νοεῖ
    Archil. fr 14.2 πόλλ' ἱμερόεντα πάθοι
    Mimn. fr 2.12 ἔργ' ὀδυνηρὰ πέλει
    Sol. fr 27.12 ἔργ' ἀπάλαμνα θέλει
    Xenoph. fr 2.18 ἔργ' ἐν ἀγῶνι πέλει

4 80 πρήγμασι γινομένους
194 χρήμασι πειθομένους (Sol. fr 4.6 χ. πειθόμενοι)
380 ἀδίκοις ἔργμασι πειθομένων
948 ἀδίκοις ἀνδράσι πειθομένους
1152 (=1238b ~ 1262), Simon. fr 92.2 Bergk ῥήμασι
   πειθόμενος
Simon. fr 140.2 Bergk λήματι πειθόμενοι
756 σώφρονι πειθόμενος
Sol. fr 13.12 ~ 4.11 ἀδίκοις ἔργμασι πειθόμενος

These parallels show us the gentleman amateur learning his art. We can readily imagine him listening to others at symposia and picking up a few handy phrases to fill out his lines and assist him in his improvisations. The assimilation will have been partly unconscious, rather like a bard learning the technique of oral poetry.[103] It would be incorrect, however, to call the poets of the *Theognidea* 'oral' poets. Their pseudo-formulae are similar to true formulae in some respects, but not in the crucial one of belonging to an extended and economic system.

Finally, in Theognis we note what may be called the 'language of lyric.' Some individual words are found in epic, but gain particular prominence in lyric because of the subject-matter (Harvey's category 5). Then there are certain things which lyric consistently describes in the same way; for example, ἐρατός and related words are very common in context of music, poetry and festivity:[104] Theognis 778 has ἐρατῆι θαλίηι, 984 τερπωλῆς ἔργ' ἐρατεινά. Cf also Archil. fr 1.2; Sapph. fr 44.32f; PLF Inc. Auct. 16.2; Alcm. PMG 10(b) 15; 27.2; Stes. PMG 278.1 (?), 2; Anac. fr eleg 2.4, PMG 373.2f; Corinna PMG 654(a) i 25. ἰρήνα ἐρατά in Alcm. PMG 1.91 is perhaps a metaphor for victory in the choral contest.[105] Again, 'flower(s) of youth' is a common expression; with the whole phrase, or just with ἥβη, the usual adjectives are ἀγλαός or ἐρατός and related words. So Theognis 985, 1007f, 1070, 1131, 1305, 1348; Archil. fr 24.14; Mimn. frr 1.4, 2.3, 5.2; Simon. fr 8.6 West; Sol. frr 4.20, 25.1; Tyrt. fr 10.28; Anac. PMG 375.1f; Bacchyl. 5.154. At Theognis 242 νέοι ἄνδρες are ἐρατοί. Alcman says that the hair of cousin Hagesichora ἐπανθεῖ like pure gold, just as Theognis 452 says that the surface of unpolluted gold has an ἄνθος καθαρόν (cf also Sol. fr 27.6 χροιῆς ἄνθος ἀμειβομένης of the fourteen- to twenty-year-old; Theog. 994 παῖς καλὸν ἄνθος ἔχων).[106]

In the only sizeable fragment of Callinus there are numerous epicisms,[107] but few actual formulae. The adjectives are all appropriate to their contexts; ὑπ' ἀσπίδος ἄλκιμον ἦτορ / ἔλσας in 10f is good; but line 7 comes close to being padded. The amount of epic diction is roughly the same as in the poetry of Tyrtaeus, but the latter has more noun-epithet combinations, which the ear perhaps notices more readily as Homeric. In these martial exhortations the poet combines in a rather loose way various arguments encouraging the soldiers to fight (eg 'the brave man wins glory,' 'fight for your wife and children,' 'death cannot be escaped,' and so on). The order in which these points occur is not very important; but Callinus does seem to have made his transitions somewhat more smoothly on the whole than Tyrtaeus.[108] The art of this fragment is also evidenced by the enjambement of lines, occasionally of couplets; Tyrtaeus is more four-square.[109]

Fragment 14 of Mimnermus may come from a poem of martial exhortation; its subject engenders a larger number of epicisms than is normal in this poet. His usual practice is to adopt a discreet number of well-chosen epithets, often adding a fine, or even exquisite, touch (eg κρυπταδίη φιλότης fr 1.3, ὀδυνηρὸν ... γῆρας fr 1.5, a phrase not found elsewhere in epic or lyric). There are no purely ornamental epithets, except those used of deities (frr 11a 1; 12.3, 10); on the other hand, he has proportionately more unaltered epic phrases than does Archilochus.

In the iambographer Semonides, the metre does not permit a large-scale use of epicisms; nor is it generally appropriate in the riotous ἴαμβος. Mock-epic is to be found in fr 7, however, as in Hipponax: lines 2 τανύτριχος, 14 πάντηι παπταίνουσα, 105 ἐς μάχην κορύσσεται. Fr 1 is a reflective piece more akin to elegy than iambus; accordingly, one finds more epic diction, so far as the metre permits: lines 1 Ζεὺς βαρύκτυπος, 14 μελαίνης ... χθονός, 15 λαίλαπι κλονεόμενοι (both epic words, although the phrase is not attested), 16 πορφυρῆς ἁλός.

At the beginning of Solon fr 4, the deities and the elevated tone of the invocation produce a concentration of epic phrases; the tone changes at line 5. The number of epithets increases dramatically also in the simile at fr 13.18ff. Elsewhere in Solon epicisms are more sparingly used, occurring at more or less regular intervals, sometimes disappearing for a few lines. His borrowings are confined to a small scale, mostly phrases of two words. He is more inclined to use the epic phrase as it is given to him than to tinker with it. Occasionally a purely ornamental epithet is used (eg πόντου ... ἀτρυγέτοιο fr 13.19, πόντον ... ἰχθυόεντα fr 13.43–5, μώνυχες ἵπποι fr 23.1). The versifier in Solon, as opposed to the poet he can also be, is further revealed by the fairly frequent occurrence of pseudo-formulae (eg frr 4.6, 11; 13.2, 16, 30, 32 [cf Tyrt. fr 12.30], 76).[110]

In the heap of epithets at the opening of fr 4 we find an example of a tendency noticed by Harvey to combine traditional epithets (ὀβριμοπάτρη, μεγάθυμος) with a new one (ἐπίσκοπος).[111] Compare further fr 13.19

πόντου πολυκύμονος ἀτρυγέτοιο; Sappho fr 44.5–7 ἑλικώπιδα ... ἄβραν
'Ανδρομάχαν; fr 44.33 Πάονα ... ἑκάβολον εὐλύραν; Ibyc. PMG 303(a)
γλαυκώπιδα Κασσάνδραν ἐρασιπλόκαμον. Something has already been said of Tyrtaeus. His subject encourages a
strong presence of the epic; his use of it to achieve a grand and stirring tone is
consistent and effective. He tends to a certain prolixity and fullness of
expression, and he has a larger number of unaltered formulae than other
poets; however, both of these traits go easily with his subject-matter. The
epic is fairly obtrusive, the poetry rarely gives the impression of patch-work.
Tyrtaeus is capable of phrases like μηδὲ φιλοψυχεῖτε, αἱματόεντ᾽ αἰδοῖα
φίλαις ἐν χερσὶν ἔχοντα, ἀσπίδος ... γαστρί, κῦμα μάχης and ἀγλαὸν
εὖχος; but in general he knows that forcefulness in his type of poetry will not
be achieved through Archilochean virtuosity.

Sappho excludes the epic fairly rigorously from her poetry, except for the
epithets of deities and a few phrases like 'black earth' (frr 1.10, 16.2; cf 'salt
sea' frr 96.10, 44.7f). This circumstance constitutes good evidence that such
phrases were felt early on to belong not only to epic but to the common
language of poetry. Among those epithets not attested in epic there is a ἅπαξ
λεγόμενον (μυθόπλοκος fr 188) and several words not found elsewhere
before Hellenistic times: φιλάοιδος fr 58.12; πολύολβος fr 133.2; ἱμερό-
φωνος fr 136 (cj. in Alcm. PMG 26.1); ἀλγεσίδωρος fr 172. There are
epithets not found in epic, but paralleled elsewhere in lyric (δολόπλοκος
of Aphrodite, fr 1.2; ἀδυμέλης fr 44.24;[112] πολυάνθεμος fr 96.11; ἀν-
θεμώδης fr 96.14), and some unique phrases:[113] χάριεν ἄλσος fr 2.2;
ποίκιλ᾽ ἀθύρματα fr 44.9; μέλος ἄγνον fr 44.26.

If the rule is that the epic is excluded from Sappho's poetry, fr 44 is the
exception that proves it. The subject (the wedding of Hector and Andromache) lends itself to the language and tone of epic. Her use of the epic is
nonetheless highly lyrical. We find traditional epithets mixed with favourite
lyric words (ἑλικώπιδα in line 5 with ἄβραν in 7; ἑκάβολον with εὐλύραν
in 33). Lyric's typical concern with music and song is reflected in the phrases
αὖλος ἀδυμέλης 24, μέλος ἄγνον 26 (cf Theog. 761 ἱερὸν μέλος), and
ἐπήρατον Πάονα 32f (see above p 45). The lists of objects in 8ff and 29f and
the colours in 8ff are also typical features of lyric.

Alcaeus has more of the epic than Sappho, and his use of epithets (as of epic
dialectal forms) is not confined to one or two poems. Instances occur
throughout his poetry; but apart from mentions of the earth, sea, ships or
deities,[114] the epic presence is still fairly limited. He has many words and
phrases unattested in epic (ἀργαλέαι ... νύκτι fr 34.11, ζακρυόεις fr 34.8,[115]
διννάεντ᾽ ... 'Αχέροντα fr 38.8, νύμφαν ἐνναλίαν fr 44.7, ποικιλόφρων fr
69.7 [elsewhere only Eur. Hec. 131], κῦδος ἐπήρατον fr 70.13, εὔδειλον

τέμενος fr 129.2 [εὔδειλος for εὐδείελος here only], ἀργαλέας ... φύγας fr 129.12, ἴρας ... ὀλυλύγας fr 130b.20, φερέσδυγον fr 249.3 [Ibyc. PMG 287.6, of a horse], μεγαλωνύμωι fr 304.3 LP [=Sapph. fr 44A Voigt], χρυσοπάστας fr 329.1, οἶνον ... μέλιχρον fr 338.6f [cf Anac. PMG 383.1f], ἄχολος and βαρυδαίμων fr 348.2, λεύκοι and ἵππιοι with λόφοι fr 140.5 = 357.3 LP, ἰόπλοκος fr 384 [3 × in Bacchyl.; cf Adesp. PMG 1001, ἰοπλόκαμος Simon. PMG 555.3], ἀφάντοις ... θυέλλαις fr 298 = s262.26f). Some of these, perhaps many, will be his own invention. His adjectives, epic and other, frequently have the vigour that characterizes his poetry in general: θυμόβορος λύα, πόλις ἄχολος καὶ βαρυδαίμων, οἶνος λαθικάδεος, ὄκνος μόλθακος, μῖσος ἄλιτρον, ἀλλαλόκακοι πόλιται.[116]

Two passages illustrate a lyric tendency, typical not only of Alcaeus, to accumulate adjectives and attributive phrases: fr 42.13f παῖδα ... [φέριστον, / ὄλβιον ξάνθαν ἐλάτηρα πώλων; fr 345 ὄρνιθες ... πανέλοπες ποικιλόδειροι ταννσίπτεροι. More accurately, it is a tendency characteristic of non-elegiac poets. The examples I have found of three or more attributive words or phrases are all from non-elegiac poets, unless Solon fr 4.3f is counted (but the invocation may be responsible): Alcm. PMG 1.48; 3.71; Stes. PMG 223.4f; Ibyc. PMG 282(a) 1f, 20ff, 34; 285.3; 303(a) 1f; Simon. PMG 543.10f; 586. Pindar and Bacchylides, too, offer a fair number of instances. This accumulative style expresses the lyric fondness of variation, detail, and ornament.[117] The reason for its absence in elegy is partly that elegists are frequently concerned to argue a point or express an opinion; in such circumstances one does not expect ornamental verbiage. Metre, perhaps, is also an important factor, for the pressure to close the sense with each couplet encourages greater concision.

In Alcman, epicisms are few and usually unstartling: νύκτα δι' ἀμβροσίαν PMG 1.62, ὕπνον ... γλυκύν PMG 3.7, αἰγλάεντος ... ὠρανῶ PMG 3.66f, βένθεσσι πορφυρέας ἁλός PMG 89.5, οἰωνῶν ταννπτερύγων PMG 89.6. (The last two belong to a passage where a stately effect is deliberately sought.) There are a few conspicuous exceptions, for which the reasons are clear: PMG 1.1ff, PMG 77 and 80 have heroic contexts; PMG 1.47ff ἵππον παγὸν ἀεθλοφόρον καναχάποδα is a simile. The rule, then, that certain situations call for epic language is well illustrated by this poet, as by Sappho in fr 44.

In his general tone, and of course in his subject-matter, Stesichorus comes closer to epic than do the other poets. He will say unabashedly τὸν δ' ἀπαμειβόμενος ποτέφα (s11.1ff), without parody as in Archilochus s478.9; hardly a line goes by without some phrase from the epic. His debt to lyric is perhaps more evident in areas other than diction. We have noted above (p 36) one example of a forthright emotional appeal; we may add the plea of Geryon's mother in s13. When Herakles returns eastward in Helios' cup, so many details are packed into a simple statement that the event is nearly obscured by the ornamentation:[118]

ἆμος δ' Ὑπεριονίδα ἲς
δέπας ἐσκατέβα ⟨παγ⟩χρύσεον ὄφρα
    δι' Ὠκεανοῖο περάσαις
ἀφίκοιθ' ἱαρᾶς ποτὶ βένθεα νυκτὸς ἐρεμνᾶς
ποτὶ ματέρα κουριδίαν τ' ἄλοχον παῖδάς τε
    φίλους,
ὁ δ' ἐς ἄλσος ἔβα δάφναισι κατασκιόεν ποσὶ παῖς
Διὸς [-υυ-].                                                                    (s17)

Similarly, these lines have rather the dazzle of lyric than the severity of epic:
        (σχεδὸν ἀν-
τιπέρας κλεινᾶς Ἐρυθείας ... )
        Ταρτησ-
σοῦ ποταμοῦ παρὰ παγὰς ἀπείρονας ἀρ-
γυρορίζους
ἐν κευθμῶνι πέτρας [υυ-υυ].                                  (s7)

Yet his diction too, which at first sight seems unaltered from epic, is characteristic of his genre. There are many epithets unattested in epic, a fair number of ἅπαξ λεγόμενα, new combinations of old epic words, expansions and other modifications of traditional formulae. For example, in s7.3f (PMG 184.2) παγαὶ ἀπείρονες is a new phrase, and ἀργυρορίζοι is a ἅπαξ; in s17.4f (PMG 185.3) ἱερά is added to the traditional νὺξ ἐρεμνά; in PMG 223.2 ἠπιόδωρος is a word once found in epic, but with μήτηρ instead of Κύπρις; in PMG 235 κοιλωνύχοι ἵπποι is unattested; in PMG 250 ἀρχεσίμολπος is a ἅπαξ; in s15 ii 5f ὀλεσάνορος αἰολοδείρου ... Ὕδρας, the first word is epic, since it occurs also in Theognis 399 (then in Nonnus), the second appears in Ibycus and then in late verse; in s89.11 εὐρύχορος is traditional, and ἁλώσιμον is likely to be epic (elsewhere in this period only Ibyc. PMG 282(a) 14, but in a heroic context), but as in the last example the combination is almost certainly Stesichorean. Instances of such lyric transformation of epic can be multiplied; their number, again, would be reduced if all epic were extant, but not drastically.

The epicisms in Ibycus, with the exception of one poem, are unobtrusive. There are very few unaltered phrases, many unattested ones, and several new epithets. In PMG 286.4 κῆπος ἀκήρατος is unattested in epic; in line 5f σκιερά is an adjective not found elsewhere with ἔρνεα, and οἰνάρεος is virtually a ἅπαξ (elsewhere only Hippoc. *Mul.* 2.195); in 10f ἀζαλέαι μανίαι is a new phrase; in line 11 ἐρεμνός is combined with ἀθαμβής, which is unattested; ἀγανοβλέφαρος in PMG 288.3 is found elsewhere only at AP 9.604.2; in PMG 298.2f ἀριστοπάτρα is new (cf ὀβριμοπάτρη), and κρατερόφρων is unattested with Athena; in PMG 321.4 ἰχθύες ὠμοφάγοι is found for ἰχθύες ὠμησταί (*Il.* 24.82); and so on.

PMG 282(a) (S151) constitutes a remarkable exception.[119] There are two reasons for the sharp increase in epic language: first, the subject-matter, which entails a parade of epic names and places; and, more importantly, the poet's ulterior motive. Ibycus is speaking of subjects for song (note δῆριν πολύυμνον line 6), and showing off his poetic skill while doing so (Μοίσαι σεσοφισμέναι line 23). 'Ibycus the poet' is the real subject; the whole execution is self-conscious and self-indulgent, like the filigree work in Liszt. If the adjectives he piles up are old and familiar, it is modern taste which finds the accumulation irksome. Moreover, if one looks closely, the transformations characteristic of lyric are only too apparent in the new combinations and modifications (ἄστυ περικλεὲς ὄλβιον, modification plus new adjective; δῆριν πολύυμνον, new phrase; Πέργαμον ... ταλαπείριον, new phrase; χρυσοέθειραν διὰ Κύπριδα, new adjective; ξειναπάταν Πάριν, new phrase, though probably epic, cf Alc. fr 283.5; Τροίας θ᾽ ὑψιπύλοιο ἀλώσιμον ἆμαρ ἀνώνυμον, new adjective [but cf Stes. S89.11], expansion; ἀρετὰν ὑπεράφανον, new phrase; κοίλαι νᾶες πολυγόμφοι, expansion; φῶτες χαλκάσπιδες new adjective; μέγας Τελαμώνιος ἄλκιμος Αἴας, expansion; χρυσόστροφος Ὕλλις, new adjective.)

By the time we reach Anacreon and Simonides, the lyric genres have come into their own and their debt to epic is virtually non-existent. Many phrases which we might have designated epic at one time have become by the end of the sixth century the property of all poets. When Ibycus says αἴ τ᾽ οἰνανθίδες αὐξομέναι σκιεροῖσιν ὑφ᾽ ἔρνεσιν οἰναρέοις θαλέθοισιν, when Anacreon says νεβρὸν νεοθηλέα γαλαθηνὸν, or when Simonides says γαλαθηνῶι δ᾽ ἤθει κνοώσσεις ἐν ἀτερπέι δούρατι τῶιδε χαλκεο-γόμφωι νυκτιλαμπεῖ, they are not evoking the epic in order to lend dignity to their composition; this is now high poetic language, theirs as much as the bards'.

It might be tempting to argue that lyric gradually became more independent of the epic during the archaic period. This could be true even of elegy, whose connections with epic were always closer than those of the other lyric genres; in Xenophanes, the last archaic elegist, there is very little epic influence. As a generalization, such a statement would be correct; some qualifications, however, are in order. We cannot be sure without the whole of lost epic before us. For all we know, epic and elegy may have developed together;[120] many phrases in Xenophanes (and in Critias for that matter) would be suitable for epic. Furthermore, we have noted that as time goes on the consciousness that a poetic word has been taken from epic disappears, so that the word becomes rather part of any poet's vocabulary. For some phrases like 'black earth' this process may have taken place very early. Much depends on how far back in the Dark Ages the origin of the lyric genres may be placed, and on how much time was required before the lyric poets felt that this diction was their own. Unfortunately, both questions are matters of speculation. At the end of the Dark Ages, we certainly find lyric poets, particularly Archilochus, in mature possession of their art.

The nature and quality of usage, as well as the subject matter, have to be kept in in mind in deciding whether elegy and lyric grew away from epic. Mimnermus' and Solon's verses have fewer epicisms than the martial compositions of Callinus or Tyrtaeus (note too what happens in Mimnermus fr 14, a poem with a Tyrtaean subject). A purely mechanical reckoning might show that Archilochus has more of the epic than Solon; but we should be obliged to note the former's ability to be completely colloquial in the elegiac metre (fr 5.3–4), his precision, and his use of the epic language for both serious and comic purposes. By a literary reckoning Archilochus is actually less indebted to the epic than is Solon, by virtue of the quality of his usage; in this sense also he less indebted than the minor poets whose work appears in the *Theognidea*.

Even in elegy, which was generally influenced by the epic, it is easy to detect an increase in the use of epicism in certain contexts. The same is true for non-elegiac poetry. Stesichorus, writing on heroic themes in dactylo-epitrite, of course has much that is epic; Alcman before him has much less, as do Sappho and Alcaeus; Ibycus after him as well. Alcman PMG 1.1ff, Sappho fr 44 and Ibycus PMG 282(a) show a dramatic increase in the amount of epicism. For these poets, the independence from epic is nearly complete; it appears only by choice, and when they are singing of themes acknowledged to belong properly to the Ionic genre. One does not find in the Doric and Aeolic poets a thoroughgoing use of epic diction for elevation in non-heroic contexts, such as we see in the extended pieces of the Theognidean corpus. Conversely, Alcaeus shows us in the Cologne poem how it was possible to write on an epic theme while using very little formulaic diction.

Lyric, then, may be further from the epic in the beginning, and closer to it at the end of the archaic period than we think. Still, it must be true that the genre gradually developed away from the epic, in respect of diction. The simple difference in amounts of epicism in early and late archaic poetry cannot be entirely argued away. The best hypothesis is that the early lyric of the Dark Ages turned to epic for dignified language. By the end of the sixth century it had completed a long evolution in which it created its own language. Already in Archilochus the use of epic diction is too precise even to be called formulaic. Different poets at different times are more successful than others, however, and an even development towards greater precision cannot be claimed. Nonetheless Anacreon seems to represent a τέλος in this respect for the archaic period, although the tendency continues in the fifth century. If at first the words lyricists were working with came mainly from the epic, a prolonged collective effort was bound in time to create a new vocabulary, so that in the end they could say with Pindar:

'Ομήρου ... μὴ τριπτὸν κατ' ἀμαξιτὸν
ἰόντες, ἀλλ' ἀλλοτρίαις ἀν' ἵπποις.

(fr 52h 11–12)

# 2

# The Organization of a Lyric Poem

The previous chapter involved us in a microscopic examination of the poems, one phrase at a time; the present chapter's point of view is more panoramic. Two questions about the structure of lyric poems will particularly concern us: do the poets employ recognizable organizational devices to arrange their material; and, can we use an understanding of these devices to solve textual and literary problems? The questions are deceptively simple; in fact, they contain a trap for the unwary. They assume that the lyric poets did indeed *want* to organize their material according to some plan which they worked out before composing their poems. It is theoretically possible that their compositions were spontaneous and disorganized, following no foreseeable direction in performance. Intrinsically unlikely as that possibility may seem, some scholars have nonetheless declared it true. It is perhaps tempting to suggest that this claim springs from philologists' characteristic inability to understand the literary art of poems; instead of patiently learning the poetry's secrets, they have prematurely declared it deficient. Yet to dismiss this view out of hand would be wrong, since it has been argued with great force and ingenuity by a scholar of acknowledged literary sensibility, Hermann Fränkel. Once again, therefore, we find ourselves engaged by his views. They are worth examining in detail, both for their merit and because of the pervasive influence they continue to exert.

On the subject of lyric structures, Fränkel seems able to claim the impressive support of Aristotle. Λέξις εἰρομένη is a phrase used by him (*Rhet.* 3.9 1409a24) to describe early (let us say, pre-Sophistic) prose. If you asked most scholars what Aristotle meant by the 'strung-on' or 'continuous' style, they would reply that it contrasts with the 'periodic' or 'rounded' style (λέξις κατεστραμμένη) in the same part of the *Rhetoric*, and refers to the mainly paratactic nature of early prose. Sentences often consist of a series of principal clauses: 'and ... and ... and,' rather like the way a child tells a story. Such an interpretation of Aristotle's words is correct in nearly all cases,[1] and can be confirmed by the style of authors like Pherecydes and Hecataeus. For convenience we may adopt here also the simple identification of λέξις εἰρομένη and 'parataxis.'

Now it is observable that parataxis is the rule in most early poetry as well. Accordingly, some scholars extend Aristotle's remarks to include poetry, although there is no actual mention of poets in this passage of the *Rhetoric*. They extend his remarks also to include the structure of entire poems, maintaining that an analogy can be drawn between the parts of a sentence and the parts of larger units: in the non-periodic sentence, cola are strung together with no regard for the overall direction of the sentence, and in the pre-classical poem, the parts are tacked on to one another in no pre-determined order.

The explanation given for the existence of such a style is a psychological one. The mind of the early Greek, like that of primitives, was obsessed with the particular, the concrete, and the sensual. Some object would seize its attention and hold it exclusively; a tangential and arbitrary association then brings another object into the periphery of vision, which claims attention in its turn. The mind becomes absorbed by this new plaything, and the first is forgotten. Incapable of disentangling itself from the particular, the early mind could not adopt a larger point of view or consider more than one thing at a time. That is why archaic poems have no coherent structure, no organic unity. Their 'unity' consists rather in the unbroken succession of particular parts, each one connected to the last by some, usually arbitrary, association. The audience is swept along from beginning to end, and interest is always maintained, but the impression of unity such poems give is only an illusion.

A few representative quotations will make this point of view clear.

The primitive mind resembles the mind of a child in that it occupies itself with the object immediately before it rather than with anything more remote.[2]

*Lexis eiromene* reflects a mind following up, one by one, the data of its subject, depicting them from a short distance and, therefore, with great intensity but without broader survey.[3]

... tous les procédés employés à la fois ne réussiront même pas à condenser en une unité vivante et organique une matière qui ne possède pas cette unité à l'état latent; seul le possible se réalise. Mais, même dans ce cas, l'emploi de procédés composition-nels adéquats forme une unité factice; il y a au moins apparence et, chez un auteur habile, forte illusion d'unité ... Les auteurs grecs archaïques sont même des hommes qui s'intéressent passionnement à leur matière et celle-ci les emporte souvent dans une direction imprévue ou paradoxale. Elle les séduit aux digressions, à un éloignement de plus en plus prononcé de la direction primaire, à un ordre arbitraire, inspiré par des associations momentanées ... [4]

Unter dieser Stilart versteht man im Satzbau das parataktische Aneinanderreihen von untereinander völlig gleichwertigen Hauptsätzen. Diesen Begriff auf den Bau grösserer Einheiten übertragend, kann man auch da von einer λέξις εἰρομένη sprechen, wo es sich um ein Aneinanderreihen von ganzen Abschnitten oder Episoden handelt ... Dieses den damaligen Stil beherrschende Prinzip der Stoffsammlung schließt a priori einen unseren Begriffen nach planmäßigen Aufbau solcher Konglomerate aus ... [5]

Several objections may be made. First, Aristotle. With the statement, 'Most sentences in Hecataeus are paratactic,' the philosopher would agree, and we can observe the truth of it for ourselves. If however one argues from this premise that Hecataeus' sentences are disorganized and illogical, or that his narrative follows no pre-determined plan, one is on much shakier ground. It is not legitimate to claim from Aristotle that the λέξις εἰρομένη does not have all the characteristics of its opposite, the λέξις κατεστραμμένη; and that because the periodic style is very logical, the non-periodic style is totally illogical. Aristotle's few remarks on the latter are vague and very general, and form part of a schematic analysis. They are meant largely as foil for the discussion of the periodic style which is his main interest. In other words, the remarks about λέξις εἰρομένη have more negative value, as a description of what the periodic style is not, than positive value, as a description of any other type of style. Beyond the simple statement that early style is usually paratactic, Aristotle offers no help if we want to know its qualities and virtues. In particular, if one tries to apply his remarks to Herodotus, an unfair judgment of that most sophisticated author is certain to result. [6]

The claim that a succession of clauses must be illogical if the connectives are principal conjunctions is questionable enough. It is even more doubtful that an analogy exists between the sentence and the structure of whole poems or prose narratives. (At this point it is fair to say also that Aristotle's support can no longer be claimed; at the most, his remarks may be applied to groups of sentences, since his topic is λέξις.) Many simple devices exist which require no great degree of logical development. Ring-composition, antithesis, and parallelism, the placing of a general statement of the poem's content at the outset as a heading, to be followed by the details, or straightforward chronological order, are perhaps the more obvious ones, and can be illustrated again and again from the archaic poets. They are simple, but they are logical. One does not need to be Isocrates to use them. To call a poetic style 'illogical' raises justifiable suspicions. Even if we can agree (as I do not think we can) that logical abilities are not found in early writing, one wonders if the criticism is not misplaced for a different reason. To take a musical analogy, the structure of Chopin's third Sonata can be and has been criticized for formlessness in comparison with a Beethoven sonata; but critics of this persuasion do not realize that Chopin's sonata creates its own rules, and wins the listener's allegiance entirely on its own terms. To speak of 'illogicality' is to demand that lyric poetry conform to irrelevant criteria. Its own peculiar ways of proceeding reflect not some psychological inadequacy in the poets, but the nature of the poetry itself.

The theory of early poetic style here discussed had its beginnings in a characteristically perceptive article by Hermann Fränkel in 1924.[7] Fränkel noticed a lot of relevant facts, but he got the explanation wrong. For example, it is true that lyric poets frequently make abrupt transitions. The reason is not that they are suddenly seized by a new, unanticipated thought; it is because such a method is appropriate to the genre. In telling you a story, the lyric poet does not proceed step by logical step, but selects highlights, and employs a highly allusive narrative technique to make the poetry evocative and forceful. Connections are not ignored; they may be unexplained, but they are often suggested, even if only in very few words. Again, it is true that lists of objects are common in lyric poetry; but this is not the result of a psychological inability to notice more than one thing at a time. The sensual naturally predominates in the lyric genre.

Two objections can therefore be made against Fränkel and his followers: they fail to make sufficient allowance for the demands of the genre; and they fail to appreciate the full extent to which organizational devices are employed. These devices argue for a certain degree of logical ability in early poets, and show that, rather than having mental operations which are of a fundamentally different order from those of later Greeks, they have fundamentally the same ways of thinking, only in a simpler and less developed form.

What one thinks on these topics makes a difference when it comes to analysing poems. Fränkel cannot fail to notice that Sappho fr 1, for example, is a powerful piece of writing. The repetition of the prayer at the end is rendered extremely effective by the intervening description of the epiphany, whose function is to show the extraordinary nature of Sappho's relation to Aphrodite. Fränkel says that the cohesion and unity of this poem do not arise from the poet's own art. It is the traditional prayer-form, demanding as it does the repetition of the prayer, which gives the poem such unity as it has;

Sappho herself, if unconstrained by the demands of the tradition, would have been content to dwell on her memory of the epiphany, getting farther and farther away from the original point. But to give all the credit to the tradition, and none to the author, is surely no satisfactory account of the poem. The picture of Sappho becoming hopelessly sidetracked, and wrenching herself back to the main argument by a sudden recollection of the demands of tradition, is thoroughly implausible. We may ask, moreover, who it was that invented and perfected the traditional form of hymns and prayers, if not the poets.

Similar judgments on the role of structural devices such as ring-composition can be found in Fränkel and his followers, who readily acknowledge their presence in the poetry, if not the extent of their use. Since they believe that the poets are incapable of giving their work a coherent structure, and are forever being seduced by the glitter of things into unanticipated digression, they say that these organizational devices were needed to keep the poets from going astray. They act as a check against the tenacity of the vivid particulars with which the archaic mind is fascinated. Now this is a strange explanation; it suggests that poets use these devices somehow in spite of themselves. It seems to imply that they would freely abandon them if given the opportunity. Yet again, it is the poets who, if they did not invent the devices, employed them frequently and with complete confidence.

To be fair, Fränkel himself thought that the 'illogicality' of archaic poetry was the result not of psychological inability or inadequacy, but of poetic preference. Homer (he well observes!) proceeds in an orderly manner, taking the time to explain the connections between things and to describe the background; so unless mankind suffered a reversion in its mental development between Homer and Archilochus, there must be some other explanation for the apparent lack of organization in lyric poems. Fränkel thought the answer lay in the discovery of the individual and of the world of inner thought at the beginning of the 'Lyric Age,' a discovery about which we learn more from Bruno Snell. Only recently, the Greeks had come to distinguish phenomena of the outside world from inner perceptions of or reactions to such phenomena. They now busied themselves with studying this relationship of inner and outer, and were led naturally to a preoccupation with the particular feeling or experience. The adoption of a paratactic world-view, if you like, was deliberate.

We have had occasion already to contest the idea that the Greeks 'discovered the mind' in the seventh century; here we may wonder with G. S. Kirk[8] whether such a thing as a paratactic world-view can ever have existed. It is a vague enough concept, and the frame of mind supposed to characterize it is really beyond our comprehension; indeed, it may be doubted if anyone ever understood it, even those supposed to have possessed it. For it is incredible that human beings ever failed to impose some kind of order on the data of their experience. It probably does not make much difference if one claims that such a failure occurred through preference rather than inability. Fränkel consistently spoke as if the poets were incapable of extricating themselves from the particular, behaving as they because they could not do otherwise. He tried to argue that it was a matter of preference, but the attempt is not convincing.

Fränkel also thought that he was rescuing the lyric poets from the mistaken judgment of some contemporaries, who regarded archaic lyric as a poor, undeveloped version of classical poetry, and therefore not worth much attention. The art of every age, he argued, has its own unique merits, which cannot be appreciated if it is judged by what it has not yet become. This is an admirable point of view and, ironically, similar to the considerations urged above. Again, Fränkel was led by such thoughts to make many valuable observations about the qualities of archaic lyric; however, his general explanation of the period's style remains open to objection. Not yet entirely free of post-Romantic ideas, he was too ready to psychologize, to find explanations for the phenomena of a text in the mind of the poet. In this attitude he was not of course alone among his contemporaries. We are more wary now of drawing such inferences between text and author. Nor is it too far-fetched to relate Fränkel's theory to the view that 'mythical thinking' precedes 'rational thinking,' and that the two are of a fundamentally different order. Ultimately this view goes back to the theories of Lévy-Bruhl, which anthropologists have not believed for a long time now. In classical studies these theories have been more tenacious. Although nearly twenty years ago G.E.R. Lloyd showed their inadequacy for the study of Greek philosophy,[9] their influence on the interpretation of Greek literature has not yet been wholly eradicated. The idea of a special primitive mentality involves the supposition that human thought developed from one state to its exact opposite; in the present case, from the supremely carefree disorganization of the archaic period to the balanced discipline of the fifth century. Most will find it easier to suppose that the development of thought from archaic to classical times was rather from the simpler to the more complex.[10]

It is time to get down to cases. I shall begin with a detailed study of the Cologne Alcaeus (fr 298). Prior to the discovery of the Cologne papyrus,[11] we had only an excerpt from the middle of the poem (Alc. fr 298 LP). It was unknown whether the myth there related had a specific purpose, or was only being told for its own sake. We now know that it was an exemplum applied to contemporary politics.[12] If we can judge by the force with which it is told, the poet never forgets the point of his story.

The narrative illustrates many of the typical patterns of lyric. At the outset the poet says (in effect): 'It would have been better for the Achaeans had they stoned Ajax; otherwise they would not have encountered the storm at Aegae.' He then proceeds to tell what Ajax did to deserve stoning, and why this affected the fleet's safety. The lines paraphrased above serve as a sort of 'heading' for the narrative: a general statement of the argument, which is then followed by supporting details.[13] The device is quite common. In Sappho fr 16, the first stanza gives the heading in the form of a priamel,[14] which is then reinforced by πάγχυ δ' εὔμαρες σύνετον πόησαι πάντι τοῦτο. The demonstration begins at line 6; here as often the particle γάρ indicates that this stage has begun. Alcaeus fr 208 (= 326 LP) begins ἀσυννέτημι τῶν ἀνέμων στάσιν, and continues τὸ μὲν γὰρ ἔνθεν κῦμα κυλίνδεται, τὸ δ' ἔνθεν κτλ. Other examples are pointed out below.[15] Although it is a simple device, the heading indicates an ability to distinguish the general from the particular. It also shows that all statements are not, as Fränkel claimed, of equal weight in archaic poems.

After the heading, Alcaeus introduces Cassandra directly. The transition seems abrupt, but the poet is merely launching into his narrative without ado. It is the same when Pindar hangs a myth on a relative pronoun. At the beginning of the narrative, or a clearly defined section of the poem, such a strategy is legitimate; the poet has the right to choose his starting-point, and the audience musts simply attend that decision. This is quite different from making an unmotivated or confusing change of direction *within* the narrative. Such a discourtesy to the audience is rarely if ever found in lyric.[16]

After describing Cassandra's situation the poet shifts his attention to the scene of carnage in the streets. The digression seems irrelevant at first, but it soon becomes clear that the rampage and noise outside the temple are meant to contrast with the lonely figure of Cassandra within.[17] The juxtaposition suffices to paint a stirring picture, done with perfect economy, but lacking nothing in force. Consider too the order in which the information is presented. Cassandra, as heroine, is brought on stage immediately, so that the audience's expectations are aroused. There is a slight lull while the focus of attention changes, to the Greeks outside;[18] then in line 16 one of their number emerges: Αἴας δὲ λ]ύσσαν ἦλθ' ὀλόαν ἔχων. If the order were Greeks – Cassandra – Ajax, the effect would not have been as striking.

From line 16 onward the poet is concerned to emphasize the heinous nature of Ajax's crime; the narrative reaches its emotional peak. As he relates the successive stages of Ajax's actions, the poet does not allow us to forget the goddess. The following scheme makes this clear:

Αἴας δὲ λ]ύσσαν ἦλθ' ὀλόαν ἔχων
ἐς ναῦο]ν ἄγνας Πάλλαδος ἀ θέων
θνάτοι]σι θεοσύλαισι πάντων
αἰνο]τάτα μακάρων πέφυκε.
χέρρεσ]σι δ' ἄμφοιν παρθενίκαν ἔλων
σέμνωι] παρεστάκοισαν ἀγάλματι
ὔβρισσ'] ὀ Λόκρος,
     οὐδ' ἔδεισε
παῖδα Δ]ίος πολέμω δότερραν.

The fact of the matter, ὔβρισσε (or whatever the precise supplement) ὀ
Λόκρος, is saved until the end, and comes like a shot. Alcaeus makes the
whole narrative as gripping and shocking as possible; the purpose, as we now
know, was to emphasize the criminality of Pittacus.

At lines 24ff there is a difficulty in the text which I have discussed
elsewhere.[19] Up to this point, our two manuscripts coincide comfortably; but
here the Cologne papyrus is reduced to fragmentary line-beginnings, and for
three lines there are gaps between the few letters supplied by the Cologne
text and the ends of the lines given by the Oxyrhynchus text.

       ]ν· ἀ δὲ δεῖνον ὐπ' [ὄ]φρυσιν (PColon. and POxy.)
25 – σμ[    ]|π[ε]λ[ι]δνώθεισα κὰτ' οἴνοπα (PColon.|POxy.)
   – ..[ ].[πόν]|το[ν] ἐκ δ' ἀφάντοι[ς
   – ἐξαπ[ίν]|ας ἐκύκα θυέλλαις.

   – αιδη.[
   – ιραισ.[
30 – Αἴας 'Αχα[ι-
   – ἄνδρος[

   ..μο[
   ..ρ.[
   ἔβασκε [
35 παννυχιο[

   πρωτοι.[
   δεινα.[
   αἴξἐποι[
   ω.σεβι.[

Unfortunately it has proved impossible to find an acceptable supplement for
line 25, even though the physical conditions of the manuscript are such that

one ought to be available. In my earlier discussion I had proposed a solution which moved lines 25–7 of the Oxyrhynchus papyrus down opposite lines 33–5 of the Cologne papyrus, while retaining the obelized lines in the latter; Page had also suggested the same alignment, but had discarded the obelized section. Ludwig Koenen in the meantime has pointed to a consideration that invalidates both solutions. The supplements to the left of the Oxyrhynchus papyrus further up in the poem are all quite regular (six letters), but both the solutions proposed have nine letters in lines 34 and 35 (ἔβασκε πόν|τον and παννυχί|οις, the second iota being slightly to the left of the τ of πόντον in the papyrus).[20] It seems then that the lines must be arranged as printed above; yet the gap between σμ- and πελιδνώθεισα remains as intractable as ever. There may be a deeper corruption than we can detect. Furthermore, we still do not know if the obelized section was an alternative version of lines 32–9, and should be ignored, or whether the lines were obelized for some less serious reason and should be retained. Many of the reasons given in the scholia for the obelization of Homeric lines are not at all compelling. In the latter case we may suppose that the suspicious repetition of ἄιξε πόντον in line 38 (ἄιξε being fairly certainly restored in line 26) refers to a secondary stage in the storm, perhaps the activity of Poseidon.[21]

If the obelized lines are retained, it means that the poet changed the setting from inside the temple to the high seas in the midst of the storm in the space of one line. This is a very abrupt transition, and one of the features of the text that prompted me to look for new solutions to the problem. As much as we hear of abrupt transitions in lyric poetry, this type is, I believe, unparalleled. The abruptness arises from the poets' technique of selecting only the highlights of a narrative important for their immediate poetic purposes. The poets are nonetheless careful to indicate the motivations of statements and actions in their poems, even if only the briefest of hints is provided (see below on Sappho fr 44). They do not set out deliberately to confuse the audience.

If the obelized lines are rejected, the first certain reference to the storm is still seven lines away at line 38. There is room in between for the poet to describe the embarkation of the fleet. I suppose the description of the scene in the temple ends at line 23, with the frightening statement 'he had no fear of the child of Zeus, giver of strength in war.' The audience shudders in anticipation; the poet builds the suspense as he describes the departure of the fleet, the crossing of the Aegean, and the approach to the fateful promontory.

However, where the text is uncertain, we must suspend judgment. In any event, the poet eventually describes the storm, thus coming full circle to the point adumbrated in the heading. We have therefore an example of the well-known pattern called 'ring-composition.'[22] In our terminology, it may be defined simply as the repetition of the heading. Such repetition is an entirely natural way of indicating the end of any discourse. In a narrative composition, where the structure of the tale often makes the end apparent, repetition is not always found; but in two circumstances it is virtually unavoidable. The first occurs when some thesis is to be argued. The speaker states what will be proved (the heading), then presents arguments, and naturally ends by repeating the opening statement as the conclusion ('QED'). The second is found when the discourse forms a digression within a larger whole. Repetition shows that the digression has been completed, that the speaker has picked up where he left off and will proceed to the next step in his original argument. Ring-composition is perhaps one of the most obvious and psychologically natural ways of organizing material, and yet not so highly structured that it would be inappropriate to an orally delivered composition. Indeed, one will hear examples in any normal conversation, and the psychological motivations outlined above (summary and progression) recur in the Greek particle combination μὲν οὖν.

Fränkel and his followers offer, as I have said, an odd explanation of ring-composition and other devices; the poets, they think, use them as a protection against their natural tendency to irrelevant digression. That this effectively puts the matter backwards is evident from Fränkel's discussion of Simonides' poem to Scopas. The saying of Pittacus, remarks Fränkel, 'was a programmatic opening to the poem; but there followed the address to Scopas, and from that Simonides had somehow to return to his theme.'[23] He did so by repeating the saying; not exactly a case of ring-composition, but the principle is the same. The question arises: why did Simonides want to get back to his main argument at all, if the archaic mind renounced such logical procedures? The same question may be put every time ring-composition is found in archaic lyric. If there were only a few examples, Fränkel's explanation might be sound; but the device can be illustrated over and over again. There are elaborate rings within rings in Homer, Pindar, and Herodotus, and the pattern is so far conventional in the Homeric Hymn to Apollo that an original subject can be taken up after a ring of some fifty lines by means of a pronoun alone (line 354). It seems that poets do have a main argument, and stick to it.[24]

In Alcaeus' poem, the recounting of the storm completes the ring which began with the heading. The mythological section ends; the poet then turns his attention to Pittacus (line 47).[25] It is an almost irresistible supposition that this application of myth to history had been adumbrated in the lost first part of the poem. The structure would then be: 'Pittacus is dangerous, and needs to be eliminated; if he is not, we will all be dragged down with him; so it would have been better for the Achaeans had they destroyed Ajax ... and thus Ajax was punished with the Achaeans; O Pittacus ...' Technically, we should say that this structure is a ring within a ring; but that makes it sound more complicated than it is, the poem's direction being immediately clear and its point entirely forceful.

Finally, we may point out that the mythological portion of the poem proceeds in chronological order: sack – rape – trial – punishment; but perhaps this does not count as an organizational device in the same way that patterns like ring-composition do. On the other hand, it has been argued that a certain order is inevitably imposed on the data of experience by the human mind. Ordering events in time is an example of this general characteristic. It may be done almost unconsciously, but ring-composition too can be employed without much conscious effort. Interestingly, Fränkel argues that archaic Greeks did *not* have the same sense of time that we do.[26] The way in which the tempo of the narrative changes in many archaic poems shows that their sense of time was not absolute. The poets speed up when events speed up, slow down when they slow down, and stand still for descriptions. It is, however, only an inference that such changes of tempo indicate a relative indifference to time. After all, the poets are unlikely to do the opposite: slow down when events quicken, and so on.[27]

As a model case, the Cologne Alcaeus has served us well. One reason is its relative length and state of preservation, and as a general consideration it must be emphasized that many archaic poems are too short or fragmentary to allow profitable discussion of their structure and organization. Often, as we shall see, additional information would readily clarify obscurities, and it is rash to conclude, on the basis of our sorry bits, that a poem is formless. When by good fortune we have a poem of any length, we usually find that some simple, clear plan is discernible.

I shall now comment on some other Alcaic fragments, and then on poems by Sappho and Alcman, before pausing to assess the results. These three poets are discussed first since, according to Fränkel, the pure λέξις εἰρομένη no longer existed after their time. Archilochus' genius makes him something of an exception; and Tyrtaeus offers special problems (fr 12 may be spurious, fr 11 may be heavily interpolated, and the organization of fr 10 cannot be discussed before the organization of others is well understood, since some scholars regard it as two poems.) Fränkel includes Stesichorus with Ibycus in the 'new school' (*Dichtung und Philosophie* 319), and neither Stesichorus (owing to the state of the fragments) nor Semonides (despite the length of fr 7) offer much to discuss from the present point of view. If I can prove the case for consistently coherent composition in Alcman and the Lesbians, the others follow *a fortiori*.

Alcaeus fr 38a. The fragment begins with an injunction, 'drink,' which serves also to give the poem's general content and purpose (a heading). Then, says the poet, *carpe diem*, for we all must die; there follows a well-chosen exemplum, which proves the point by an *a fortiori* argument; the sense of line 10 seems to be the same as in line 4, 'do not hope for such things,' so that we have a ring. All is perfectly clear, and the structure is intellectually satisfying.

Fr 42.   ἔστι τις λόγος is a known method of beginning a tale,[28] but I know of no parallel for ὡς λόγος used in this way.[29] It is likely, therefore, that this myth was used as an exemplum; the poem ends with it, suggesting that the truth it embodies lives on.[30] The fragment as we have it forms a ring beginning and ending with Helen. Peleus and Thetis are in the middle; the transition back to Helen by way of Achilles gives the fragment a neat cohesion.

Fr 129.   The fragment owes a certain amount to prayer-form, but it clearly has a literary, not a purely religious, purpose. Although Alcaeus is sincerely praying, the form is a peg on which to hang the story of Pittacus' treachery. There may have been a repetition of the prayer in lines 9ff at the end, which would tie the whole composition together. In the intervening section, note that the whole of lines 14–24 is an explanation of lines 13f τὸν ῎Υρραον δὲ παῖδα πεδελθέτω κήνων 'Ερίννυς.[31]

Fr 130b.   It is probable that a new poem begins at line 16 of the papyrus (Page, *Sappho and Alcaeus* 200f); it is unfortunate, then, that the text is full of holes, because we might have had a complete poem. The opening lines seem to ramble somewhat, but if Page (ibid 204) is right (as he surely is) in taking τά in line 5 as the antecedent of ἀπὺ τούτων in 8, the organization is tighter. Onymacles in line 9 seems to be a hermit-figure; if so, this refers back to line 2 and forms a ring. After line 10 all is inscrutable; Alcaeus arrives at the sanctuary, and he expatiates on the beauty contests which take place there. What role if any this topic plays in the poem, we do not know. The function of the apparently gnomic statement in lines 11f is also unclear. At line 21 the text deserts us entirely.

Fr 347.   Fränkel says that while Hesiod is fuller and more elegant, Alcaeus' poem is sharper and more urgent.[32] Hesiod's τῆμος ... ἦμος has been replaced by a simple γάρ. At any rate, the poem is clearer. Hesiod advises a number of other activities besides drinking, and takes his time doing so; Alcaeus puts the point at the outset as a heading, and does not obscure it with extraneous material. The γάρ indicates, as usual, that the heading is followed by the argument.

Fr 140 (357 LP).   G. Maurach has noted that all of the details in lines 1–7 are not equally weighted, as Fränkel argued.[33] There is an increase in tempo throughout; each successive piece of armour receives less description. The effect of the last line, τῶν οὐκ ἔστι λάθεσθαι, is thereby increased, since it is made to seem a climax.

The fragment also illustrates a device found elsewhere, in which the two sections of a poem are either complementary (a long first section provides the background to or explanation of a point expressed in the shorter section) or antithetical. For this phenomenon I shall use the terms 'protasis' and 'apodosis.' Because of the rhythm (long versus short), the 'apodosis' gains in emphasis. A clear example is Theognis 237–54. The first sixteen lines expatiate on the poet's gift to the boy; the final couplet then emerges with full force:

> αὐτὰρ ἐγὼν ὀλίγης παρὰ σεῦ οὐ τυγχάνω αἰδοῦς
> ἀλλ' ὥσπερ μικρὸν παῖδα λόγοις μ' ἀπατᾶις.

Sappho in fr 2 describes the grove at some length (three stanzas), then says ἔνθα δὴ σὺ ... Κύπρι. For fr 16, see below n 38. Her prayer to Aphrodite might also be considered an example of the same device, since the repetition of the prayer required by the traditional form is rendered much more effective by the length as well as the nature of the preceding description of the epiphany. We may compare also the structure of Alcman PMG 89: εὕδουσιν δ' ὀρέων κορυφαί τε καὶ φάραγγες, five lines, εὕδουσιν δ' οἰωνῶν φῦλα τανυπτερύγων, one line; and of Alcman PMG 16: 'he was not a rustic nor an oafish man, nor ... of Thessalian blood, nor an Erysichean shepherd' four lines, '(he came) from high Sardis' slightly more than one line. See further below on Sapph. fr 94; Archil. fr 4.6ff; fr 19; Theog. 221–6, 769–72, 783–8, 891–4; Simon. fr 8 West; Sol. fr 36; Tyrt. fr 12; Ibyc. PMG 282(a); and Anac. PMG 388.

## SAPPHO

Fr 1.   Something has already been said of this poem above (pp 56f). The first stanza alone shows how vibrant the traditional form is in this artist's hands: λίσσομαί σε is very urgent, the request intimate and personal. ἀλλὰ τυίδ' ἔλθε in line 5 is an expression infused with Sappho's own values: the coming of Aphrodite means comfort. Yet it is the non-traditional parts of the poem that are really remarkable. Some past action of the deity or some past service of the suppliant is conventionally described, but the length of the description here is unprecedented.[34] It is also an epiphany. The narrative is not an impersonal or factual account, but the expression of all that the goddess means to Sappho. The effect is to render the conventional repetition of the request (ἔλθε μοι καὶ νῦν, line 25) far more forceful than it otherwise may have been. Scholars who complain that the epiphany has been allowed to go on to the point of irrelevance³⁵ fail, I think, to apprehend what the poem would be like without it. 'Come to me now too,' says Sappho; the statement is lifeless without the full explanation of what that visitation will mean. The poem exhibits, as it is commonplace but nonetheless necessary to say, that harmony of form and content which characterizes disciplined art.

Fr 16. The poem, so far as we have it, offers a clear structure: the first stanza states the heading; stanzas two to four provide proof in the form of a mythological exemplum; the fifth stanza repeats the opening argument, 'QED.' The poet's argumentative stance is apparent from her words in line 5f, πάγχυ δ᾽ εὔμαρες σύνετον πόησαι πάντι τοῦτο.

Fränkel, in keeping with his views on λέξις εἰρομένη, observes that the exemplum proves too much.³⁶ Page complains that it is 'inelegant' of Sappho, having said that τὸ κάλλιστον is what one loves, and proposing to prove this by reference to Helen's love, to say that Helen herself was most beautiful of mortals.³⁷ Neither objection affects the structure of the poem. But we may wonder whether these objections are justified. It is true, as Page says, that the logic of the comparison will not stand up to close scrutiny, but this is hardly disturbing, except to an excessively rationalistic critic. Having thought of Helen as the most obvious proof of her dictum, Sappho can scarcely avoid mentioning that woman's beauty, since Anactoria, who is to her exceptionally beautiful (17ff), is already very much in her mind at this point. ἀ ... πόλυ περσκέθοισα κάλλος ἀνθρώπων in lines 6–7 can be applied directly to Anactoria. Helen therefore does double duty: she is like Sappho in the power of her love, and she is like Anactoria in her beauty. No one will perceive any conflict between these two functions, unless the poem is analysed with too rigorous logic, which is to say, inappropriately analysed. The poem proceeds by a typically lyric association of ideas. The power of love in general, the qualities of one famous love, the pain of separation, and the allure of beauty all combine in the consciousness of poet and audience, when the poet finally declares (15f):³⁸

ἄ] με νῦν Ἀνακτορί[ας ὀ]νέμναι-
σ᾽ οὐ] παρεοίσας.

Fr 31. Of all Sappho's poems this is the most controversial. Fortunately, an exhaustive analysis with very promising results has recently been published by Emmet Robbins.³⁹ According to him, the poem is to be articulated thus: 'That man seems to me equal to the gods, who sits opposite you, and hears your talk and laughter, which [laughter] throws me into a panic. For when I look at you I cannot speak [etc]; [in short], I think I am dying.' The point is that the man feels no such threat to his mortality in the presence of the girl; therefore he is like the immortals who cannot die. A strong stop is to be placed after ἐπτόαισεν in line 6; γάρ in line 7 does not so much explain what immediately precedes as introduce lines 7–16 which, considered as a unit, explain lines 1–6. φαίνεται in line 1 responds with φαίνομαι in line 16 (as Wilamowitz argued).

The result of this analysis, as Robbins points out, is that the poem is composed of two nearly periodic sentences.[40] Owing to the authority and success of Fränkel's views, Robbins finds it necessary to counter the objections of those who might find an archaic poet 'incapable of such calculated effect' (261) by reference to Ibycus PMG 266 and 267. Fränkel, of course, counted Ibycus as a member of the 'new school' of lyric poets who possessed a more advanced technique than earlier writers like Sappho, and would not have allowed the parallel. If our arguments have any force Robbins can refer to any number of contemporary and earlier poems to support his interpretation.

Fr 44. The events are related in chronological sequence: the messenger speaks to the king; the king then takes action; preparations are made; the couple arrives; the celebrations begin. Throughout the poem there is an alternation of tempi. The leisurely messenger's speech is effectively contrasted with the one-line description of the king's reaction that follows. Sappho is concerned to emphasize the swift response of the king and others (ὀτραλέως 11, αὔτικα 13, where there is also an asyndeton) as an indication of the excitement prevailing. Few words are wasted in these lines, and Sappho accomplishes her purpose by selecting representative and evocative details: ἀνόρουσε of the father (line 11) says volumes. We assume naturally, though the author does not tell us, that the father gives instructions for the preparations. In 13ff, sufficient examples of the general activity are given to convey the impression of bustle. The bride and the groom arrive somewhere in the gap at lines 20ff, and then we have the feast. There is universal rejoicing; everything sparkles. The tempo has slowed down again as the poet describes the scene in detail.

Fränkel uses this poem at the outset of his article to show how lyric, unlike epic, does not provide the background to events, but keeps its gaze ever fixed on the here and now. Yet here as elsewhere alertness to the methods of lyric is required. The poets are aware of the 'background' and the connections between their statements, but do not belabour them at the expense of forcefulness. Line 12, φάμα δ' ἦλθε κατὰ πτόλιν εὐρύχορον φίλοις, indicates briefly how the whole city was fired up at the news; in particular the φίλοι got wind of it. Possessing this information, we understand that lines 13ff list individual examples of universal activity. If line 12 is omitted, line 13 seems to lack motivation; the reason for the preparation of the carts is momentarily obscure, and the transition jars somewhat. Similarly, the eagerness implied by line 12 gets its start from the father's eagerness in line 11. Lyric is always careful to provide the motivation for what is said. Read through the myth of the fourth *Pythian*, for example. In spite of the many spans of time omitted and the extreme selectivity of detail, the poet always provides sufficient information for understanding each step of the narrative, even if he does so with only the slightest of hints.

Fr 94.   Anne Burnett has made Schubart's suggestion very probable that the opening line is spoken by the departing girl.[41] On the opposite view, the description of past experiences goes on rather long for no apparent reason; we wonder when Sappho is going to return to the mood of the opening line. Being open-ended, the poem falls flat. With the opening line restored to its original speaker, however, there is no puzzling conflict of moods and no difficulty with the structure. Sappho's response is self-contained; its purpose is to describe with simple elegance and candour the things that made life meaningful to her and her circle: beauty, love, their identity as a group, worship, and memory. Burnett stresses that the details of the poem are not randomly put down but proceed in a very logical order: the girl's ornaments are described from the head down (the perfume would have been poured on the breast); the erotic undertone of these lines leads well to the mention of the couch in line 21; then the individual act of love is placed in the context of the group's worship. Doubtless the poem ended with a repeated admonition to remember old friends, and formed a ring with line 8.

Fr 96.   For Fränkel, this poem is a perfect example of how the archaic mind slides from one object to the next in unbroken succession without following any pre-planned course. The simile, though perhaps ranging no farther afield from the *tertium comparationis* than some Homeric similes, has no Homeric ὥς-formula, and that it is a simile seems to have been forgotten by the end. The moon which is the object of Sappho's imagination becomes a real moon, and the girl is imagined wandering to and fro in its light.

   First, a point of Greek. 'Wandering to and fro' is the usual translation of ζαφοίταισα in line 15. The word should mean 'going through.' The compound verb is not used absolutely before Herodotus (1.60.5), and in Homer the natural prepositions to indicate a vague 'to and fro,' 'up and down,' are ἀνά and κατά. The verb ought to have specific reference, and the supposition (made by Fränkel and others) that the girl διαφοιτᾶι the fields and flowers of 11ff is correct.[42]

The first consequence of this reading is to give the passage some degree of cohesion. If no object is supplied for ζαφοίταισα from the preceding context, then we must say that Sappho gets completely off track, finally having to end her reverie abruptly in order to get back to the subject of the poem. An important consequence also emerges from the rendering 'passing through' as opposed to 'wandering.' Fränkel and others, using the latter translation, see the progression of thought in the passage thus: girl among Lydian women; comparison of girl to moon; transfer of attention to surrounding nocturnal scene; return to girl, who is now wandering in this scene, it having been forgotten that the passage started out as a simile. Now, what has happened to the Lydian women in the meantime? Nothing, I think. The translation 'wandering' carries with it the notion that the girl is alone. It is at least as likely that in Sappho's imagination she continues to be among the Lydian women. Through the fields and flowers, and among the other women she διαφοιτᾶι as Pan διέπει the nymphs, fields, and flowers in the nineteenth Homeric hymn (line 23). If we accept that such a picture is in Sappho's mind throughout this passage, then all is understandable. She sees them all together at night. She begins with the central figure, her absent friend, whom she compares to the moon above the girl and her new companions, much as Alcman compares Agido to the sun in the sky above the chorus (PMG 1.40ff).[43] The surrounding scene is described; its beauty is certainly meant to reflect on the girl (lyric juxtaposition again). When Sappho returns to the subject of the girl, she is really completing a ring; she is thus able to pick up where she left off before the ring began, in Lesbos with the other girls. The 'illogicality' of introducing a simile and then abandoning it becomes a trifling objection, when we realize that Sappho is less composing a simile than describing what she sees in her imagination.

There is nothing in the text against this interpretation, and insistence on the correct rendering of ζαφοίταισα removes the prejudice which dictates that the girl is alone. In honesty, however, it has to be admitted that the Lydian women may have disappeared from Sappho's imagination, so that the girl is thought to be 'passing through' only the fields and flowers, alone. Moreover, the expression φοιτᾶν ... διά is a good way to describe a god's movement in a favourite haunt (hHom. 19.8, Eur. Hipp. 148); in the latter passage Barrett's translation 'ranges over' catches the nuance nicely. There is perhaps not much of a distinction between this and 'wandering.'[44] We are left therefore with two alternatives which are both, so far as conclusive evidence goes, equally likely. In support of my view, however, I may point out some probable consequences, which may find the support of some.

If Sappho pictures a group of women abroad at night, it is certain that they are engaged in some sort of cult celebration.[45] The supposition that these women are a group like Sappho's own circle in Lesbos then becomes attractive. Indeed, the occasion on which the poem was performed may have been just such a nocturnal gathering; or at least such gatherings would have been completely familiar to the audience. They would have understood Sappho's meaning as outlined above without much prompting from the poet.

There may of course have been something in the lost portions of the poem to make things clear. Indications are very slight, but in line 5 Sappho says μάλιστ᾽ ἔχαιρε μόλπαι. In 26f Aphrodite appears to have poured nectar; we have no context, but at least the passage puts us in mind of fr 2, where a similar activity is clearly part of a cult celebration. The definite article in the expression ἀ βροδοδάκτυλος σελάννα[46] (line 8) cannot be fitted into the categories of usage which, so far as they can be established, were given by Lobel.[47] He confesses (lxxiv) that exceptions to his rules are most likely to occur where the article has particular reference, as will be the case here if Sappho and her friends are themselves engaged in a nocturnal celebration; the moon of Lydia will also be the moon of Lesbos. The fields and flowers become the ones under their own feet; chervil and melilot (lines 13 f) are used in garlands in a fragment of Cratinus,[48] garlands such as the girls would certainly be wearing on the occasion of this poem if gathered for religious purposes.

### ALCMAN

PMG 1. This is the only fragment of Alcman which is of any real use from our point of view, but any advantage gained by its length is nearly eliminated by the difficulties of interpretation.[49]

Lines 1–35 contain a myth; it is likely, although not certain, that there was something in the myth that paralleled the composition of the choir(s) or was relevant in some way to the occasion of the ceremony.

At lines 36ff gnomic sentiments are used as a pivot between sections, a device which was to become conventional by Pindar's time. The next lines may be translated: 'I sing the radiance of Agido; I see her like the sun, which Agido asks to shine as our witness.'[50] One of two things must be meant: either Agido is praying for the sun to rise; or she is asking an already risen sun to notice them. The former surely jars in a Greek context; the latter is perfectly natural. As the sun rises [51] and casts its light on the girls, Agido seems to the chorus merely an extension of the heavenly radiance. Nothing could be easier for them than to compare Agido to the sun, and then suggest that beautiful Agido herself asks the sun to shine on the rest of them. Understood in this manner the passage readily withstands the objection that the sun of the simile suddenly becomes the real sun, with consequent confusion for the audience.[52] The sun of the simile *is* the real sun; as in the passage of Sappho above (p 69), the poet is not so much developing a simile as describing a scene. The expression, 'I see her like the sun [there], which she asks to shine as our witness,' is readily intelligible on normal levels of discourse; although it may actually entail a combination of several different notions, the combination is natural and effortless, and difficulties are really only discovered by the analytical mind.

After singing the praises of Agido, the chorus says 'but the splendid leader of our choir permits me neither to praise nor to blame her, for this maid stands out, just as if one were to place among the cattle a sturdy champion, a thunder-footed steed, creature of dreams beneath a rock.' In the usual interpretation of these lines, αὐτά is read in line 45, and the translation runs: 'she [Hagesichora] permits neither praise nor blame [of Agido], because she herself stands out ...' In other words, Hagesichora is jealous of her superiority. However, the poet has not said 'Hagesichora permits no praise,' but 'she permits neither praise nor blame,' a 'polar' expression which means 'to say nothing.' The point is that words are unnecessary; Agido's beauty is obvious. Agido is therefore the subject in lines 45ff; she is the champion filly. αὖτα, not αὐτά, should be read in line 45, and the meaning understood to be: 'Hagesichora permits no words, for this girl is beautiful.' The chorus would indicate Agido with a gesture, as they do Hagesichora in lines 56f, where exactly the same point is made about her: 'Why do I need to tell you in so many words? This [αὖτα] is Hagesichora.' Her beauty is obvious.[53]

This analysis yields three important results. First, the notion that Agido and Hagesichora are rivals loses any support in the text. At lines 79f we notice that they stand side by side, and at lines 57ff the chorus does not say that Agido is superior to Hagesichora or vice versa, but that both are superior to all. Throughout the poem the girls are very careful to preserve the equality of the two leaders, giving brief attention to one when the other has the limelight (44, 57f), and mentioning the two together at 77ff.[54]

Second, the transition between the two stanzas becomes much smoother. Lines 50f say: 'Do you not see? The courser is Venetian; but the hair of my cousin Hagesichora shines like gold ...' The 'courser' is Agido. According to the normal interpretation of the preceding lines, Hagesichora had been the subject, and was compared to a race-horse; now in line 50 we suddenly switch back to Agido, although the comparison is still, suspiciously, to a horse (to which Agido is again compared in 58f). Then, after one line, we return to Hagesichora. In our analysis, Agido is the subject of lines 45ff, and line 50 may now be just what it sounds like, a summation of the preceding argument: 'Well, can't you see? The courser μὲν is Venetian; but as for Hagesichora ...'[55]

Finally, the discussion has some important consequences for the structure of the whole. The content of the poem is now arranged so that pauses coincide with stanzas. Some of the poems of Bacchylides and Pindar illustrate this pattern, but it is all the more pronounced in Sappho and Alcaeus, whose poems, like Alcman's, have closer affinities with folk songs, or at least with more popular, less sophisticated forms of literature.[56] The mythological portion of Alcman's poem ends with a stanza; after a gnomic pivot, virtually the whole of the next stanza deals with Agido, the one that follows with Hagesichora. Lines 60–3 form a transition to the following stanza, which deals with the girls of the chorus. Hagesichora and Agido appear again in 77–81; then another gnomic pivot in 83–4. The remainder of the poem is taken up mainly with the choir's hopes for victory under the care of their leaders. Thus: myth (5 stanzas, assuming one complete column lost in the papyrus); Agido (1 stanza); Hagesichora (1); chorus (1); leaders and chorus together, with prayers for victory (2, which produces a pattern of 5 + 5 for the whole poem). A simple enough plan, but a plan it is.

The last statement applies to all of the poems hitherto examined, and we can be confident that these three poets are in control of their material. A similar conclusion will obtain for the remaining authors. The individual discussions which follow will necessarily give the rest of the chapter a fragmentary character, but I offer them with the idea that they can be consulted selectively. Attention should, however, be directed to the discussion of the organizational devices of antithesis and balance (below p 76f), since it is important to the argument of the whole chapter.

### ARCHILOCHUS

Fränkel has adequately demonstrated the ability of this poet to organize his thoughts. He points out the way in which the fragments move from weaker to stronger expressions of the central idea, how the decisive argument is placed at the end, and how the poems are often divided into two antithetical halves.[57] I have made some observations about Archilochus' structures in Chapter 1, p 41; I offer a few additional comments here.

Fr 4.6ff. 'Come, bring the wine'; (slightly less than three lines) 'for we won't be able to stay sober on this watch' (slightly more than one line). Protasis and apodosis.

Fr 19. 'I don't like x, y, z, for they are far from my eyes.' Protasis and apodosis.

Fr 23. The similarity of this fragment to the Cologne epode (s478) needs to be noticed. In both poems, Archilochus (or the character he represents) speaks with a woman; in both, if West is right in his interpretation, the subject is erotic;[58] in both, conversational style is wonderfully affected; both use high-flown language for comic effect.[59] The text preserved of fr 23 falls roughly into two halves, 8–16 devoted to the speaker, and 17–21 devoted to the addressee; but within each section the conversational style, and perhaps also the speaker's agitation, produce a somewhat bumpy sequence of thought.

Fr 122.  Line 5 is a heading for lines 6–9.

Fr 130.  Whatever lies concealed in τοῖς θεοῖς †τ'εἰθεῖάπαντα, it is evidently a heading.

The Cologne Epode (S478). Cf on fr 23. Again, if the poem seems to proceed rather bumpily, this is the result of its conversational style. Note, however, that the seducer manages carefully to answer every point raised by the girl:[60]
    1–2: The girl seems to be urging restraint; in 19–21 he promises it (though of a different kind).
    3: εἰ δ' ὦν ἐπείγεαι καί σε θυμὸς ἰθύει: he replies with a twist, that he's in no rush – to get married (13ff; ἐπ' ἡσυχίης, 16); and throws the same charge of haste back at the girl's sister (39ff).
    6f: The sister is supposed to be beautiful; this is rebutted in detail at 26ff.
    8: The girl advises Archilochus to take her sister; he replies that everybody else does (38).

The Strasbourg Epode (Hipponax fr 115 West). Fränkel, who regards the poem as Archilochean, says that the way in which the motivation for the long curse is held back until the end is typical, although he admits that the occasion for this hatred may also have been related in the part of the poem now lost to us.[61] If so, the poem's structure is a ring. The striking verses which form the conclusion of the ring also conclude the poem, thus giving it special finality.

### THEOGNIS

221–6. 221–4: 'Who thinks his neighbour knows nothing is a fool, for we all have clever schemes'; (protasis) 225–6: 'the real point is to what end we use them' (apodosis).

237–54. See above p 65.

401–6. Lines 402ff give a particular example to prove the general principle expressed in 401f.

429–38. 429–31 give the theme; 432–4 an exemplum; 435–8 the theme again.

453–6. The author alternates between two sides of an antithesis three times within the structure of a conditional sentence; cf Appendix. The structure of the piece shows that it is certainly fifth century.

467–96 is a poem delivered when the symposium has been going on for some time; some of the guests have fallen asleep from the effects of the wine (469–70), some want to go home (467), and the speaker himself is about to do so (475f). He begins with negative injunctions; line 472 provides the reason. The varying length (five lines versus one) illustrates the structure of protasis and apodosis. 'Let others drink, for we don't have a party like this every night' in 473–4 introduces what the speaker intends to do (αὐτὰρ ἐγώ, 475). In 475ff the speaker says he will go home because he's had enough; this leads to a few lines on moderation, which in turn introduce a description of Simonides' behaviour (483–92) by contrast. Finally, some advice to the whole party. The structure of the lines may be described thus: ἐγώ 475–83; σύ 483–92; ὑμεῖς 493–6.

657–66. Two couplets express complementary aspects of the same thesis; 661–6 give specific examples to prove it.

667–82. The opening couplet is in a way a heading for what follows, since the speaker goes on to indicate (briefly) his situation among the ἀγαθοί (669 f) and to elaborate the reasons for his poverty. But lines 669ff are also directed to the ἀγαθοί as a warning (681); this thought is not in the first couplet.

699–718.[62] The poem is a ring; between the heading and its repetition, the argument is illustrated by a series of exempla. This is clearly the design of the poet, and the epic colour of his language probably indicates that he means this to be an elevated, seriously poetic effort (cf above, Ch 1 p 42f). However, his symmetry goes awry in the middle section when he devotes five and a half couplets to one exemplum. The loss of symmetry weakens the argument; the plan ought to have been to hammer the point home with a regularly repeated οὐδ' εἰ, as in Tyrtaeus fr 12 and Xenophanes fr 2.

This objection to the poem's effectiveness can be partly countered by two considerations. First, the digressive material is actually limited to lines

706–12, since lines 703–5 explain the character of Sisyphus' 'knowledge' mentioned in 702. Lines 706–12 form a ring whose purpose is clear: the poet wishes to emphasize the unique nature of Sisyphus' accomplishment ('no one else ever did this, because death is final; but Sisyphus returned even from the dead'). By doing so he forcefully proves the statement made in lines 699ff. At line 713 we notice that the poet continues with subordinate clauses dependent on τῶν δ' ἄλλων οὐδὲν ἄρ' ἦν ὄφελος in 700; evidently he has not forgotten his structure.

A second consideration which helps to explain the length of this section is that too much regularity seems to have been distasteful to Greek writers of all periods. Although, as Norden pointed out, formal parallelism is the hallmark of Greek style as contrasted with the parallelism of content in Hebraic writing,[63] there is a tendency in Greek, even in the earliest archaic pieces, slightly to disturb an otherwise perfect symmetry. As time goes on, more and more variety is introduced, until a sort of τέλος is reached as far as lyric poetry is concerned with Pindar. The development of prose follows a similar pattern; Gorgias' early attempts were regarded as extreme, even by Isocrates, who found it necessary to eliminate the excesses of Gorgian style in order to make it palatable to his audiences. In the two archaic pieces formally similar to the Theognidean passage under discussion, it is interesting that Tyrtaeus (fr 12) distributes the exempla in the first eight lines one to a line (except in line 2, where there are two exempla), whereas Xenophanes (fr 2.1–5) arranges his poem so that the exempla begin at a variety of places in the lines.[64] However, even if there is something of this phenomenon in the Theognidean passage, it must be admitted that we have to do not with a 'slight disturbing' of the balance but with a complete upset. We can identify the poet's purpose in writing 706–12, but this hardly justifies the space occupied by the lines in the poem as a whole. The result is a distortion of the poem's structure, and slight confusion in the reader's mind at 713. However, these features are really only faults in composition, and should be attributed to the poet rather than to the archaic age and its psychology.

731–52. The prayer falls into two halves, the first expressing the situation the speaker would like to see, the second the situation as it is. The first half, lines 731–41, is summed up at 741 with ταῦτ' εἴη μακάρεσσι θεοῖς φίλα, which is an echo of εἴθε γένοιτο θεοῖς φίλα in 731. This ring is further divided into two antithetical sections, 731–6 on bad men, 737–40 on good ones. νῦν δέ, in antithesis with ταῦτα in 741, introduces the second half; we have first a general description of the present, followed by two long rhetorical questions.

769–72. The single-line question at the end gives a reason for the advice of the previous three lines (protasis and apodosis).

783–8. Line 788 is in apodosis to lines 783–7.

879–84. πῖν᾽ οἶνον, the poem begins, as Alcaeus fr 347.

891–4. The first three lines describe the damage which the Cypselids have wrought, and which the speaker's party has been unable to prevent; this is the background (protasis) to the wish in the last line, 'Damn the Cypselids!'

903–30. A closely reasoned piece, with numerous indications of a classical origin.[65] Still, some characteristics of the archaic genre carry on, like the opening heading, and the penchant of the couplet to contain the two sides of an antithesis (913f, 925f; see below). The argument of the poem is: the man who watches his money wisely has the best ἀρετή; for, since we do not know when our life will end, there is a chance of being caught short before we die, or of leaving a lot of money behind to those whom we don't want to get it. In detail: Lines 903–4, general statement; 905–8, 'of course, if we knew when we were to die, there would be no problem'; 909–14 'but we don't, and I don't know which course to choose.' 915–19 'I have seen a man who saved all his money, and it went into the wrong hands when he died'; 920–2 'and the man who spent it all, so that he is now a beggar.' 923–8 'So keep track carefully, and neither will happen to you; you will have money in your old age, when you particularly need it.' The sentiment of 929–30 that the poor man has no friends and cannot be ἀγαθός does not belong here, and sounds like the typical Theognidean fare (cf 697f, 857ff, 299f); the couplet should therefore be separated from what precedes.

949–54. The opening paradox has one couplet to itself; it is followed by two paradoxes with one line each, then four, each with half a line. The increasing intensity is enhanced by the sharper expression of the paradox of the last two lines (πρήξας δ᾽ οὐκ ἔπρηξα κτλ.).
Antithesis is a favourite means of organizing material in this poet, as in others, and may count as another simple yet effective structural device available to writers from the beginning. It exists on the most basic level in the μὲν ... δέ construction of the Greek language. In the Theognidean corpus antithesis can be found in single lines, couplets, pairs of couplets, and in large sections such as 731–52, 905–14, and 915–22. The balance is sometimes exact in terms of numbers of lines devoted to each side of the antithesis;

other times the balance is slightly off.[66] Balanced parallelism may be cited in this connection (parallelism and antithesis being closely related, and frequently shading one into the other).[67] This matching of antithesis or parallelism with the metrical shape is so frequent that it may be recognized as a generic characteristic. Whether the metre existed first, and its shape encouraged this manner of thinking, or whether the thinking encouraged the development of the metre, we cannot say; they simply appear as correlatives from the first, existing quite happily together.

The same pressure of the metre produces an even more frequent phenomenon whereby the hexameter expresses a thought, and the pentameter amplifies it, gives the reason for it, qualifies it, or specifies the circumstances in which it is true.[68] The desire to complete a thought with the couplet is particularly evident when the pentameter is mere padding (168, 1044; cf also 242, 302, 1358). On the other hand, while there is a tendency to contain each independent thought within a couplet, it is notable that in some of the fragments, and in some elegiac poets, there is a definite tendency in the other direction: to begin new thoughts at various points in either hexameter or pentameter, or to ignore the boundary of the couplet, spreading thoughts over odd numbers of lines. So lines 441–6, 503–8, 773–88, 789–94, 903–30; Archilochus, Callinus, Critias, Dionysius Chalcus, Ion, and Mimnermus also follow the same pattern. Solon presses on a couplet at a time, except in one passage, fr 13.17–25, which is otherwise distinguished by its simile and deliberately elevated tone (above, Ch 1 n 92). Xenophanes keeps within the couplet as well, except in fr 2.1ff, where there may be other reasons for his variation (see above p 75); contrast the shorter repetition of the opening lines' content at 15–17. In the poetry of Tyrtaeus there tends to be a sense-pause at the end of every line. Enjambment of couplets may be taken as a mark of virtuosity (Archilochus) or lateness (all the fifth-century elegists have it except Euenus). Early archaic lyric has a four-square quality, while later elegy tends to flow more; comparison with sculpture is apt. This development is in keeping with the observation made above that Greek poetry likes symmetry, but not too precisely balanced or unvaried.

MIMNERMUS

Fr 1.  The fragment falls into two halves, the first on the joys of youth and love, the second on the horrors of old age.

Fr 2.  Lines 1–8 form a ring, each extremity being formed by the sentiment that youth is all too brief. Within the ring, it is said that young men 'know neither good nor evil from the gods,' ie they 'know nothing,' which is to say they are, for the time being, unmolested; but the Κῆρες of old age and death stand by. This anticipates the second half of the poem, which concentrates entirely on the evils of old age and the different sorts of death which befall us.

Fr 5.   Lines 1–3 describe the poet's reaction to a young beauty; this leads to the reflection that youth is too short.[69] The second half contrasts old age.

## SEMONIDES

Fr 1.   Lines 1–5 are a general statement of the theme which falls into two antithetical sections, 1–2 on Zeus' point of view and 3–5 on men's. Ignorance, man's principal characteristic, leads naturally to his hoping; the opening section thus introduces the next one (6–10). We hope for good things, of course, but bad things befall use; so to the next section, a list of disasters (11–22) which is unified by an extended μὲν ... δέ construction (τὸν μέν 11; τοὺς δέ etc 12, 13, 15, 18; note the variation in construction and length of each δέ-sentence.) The general statement in 20–2 sums up this section; οὕτω in line 20 is prominent, and shows that the poet has not forgotten the point of this enumeraton. A gnome advising moderation (cf Archil. fr 128, Theog. 1031ff) concludes the fragment. This note has not been sounded yet, but the topic is an integral part of the store of traditional wisdom (see above, Ch 1 p 24f) and readily suggests itself.

The poem's parts flow one into the other, a recurring feature of λέξις εἰρομένη, according to Fränkel; but the parts of this poem cohere, and the transitions seem not arbitrary but inevitable.[70]

Fr 7.   Lines 1–2 are the heading; the proof of the argument follows in the form of τὴν μὲν ... τὴν δὲ ... τὴν δέ etc, for ninety-odd lines. 94–116 is a summary section on the evil nature of women in general, all examples thus far being bad, except one. Line 96 is repeated at 115 to form a ring. The poet evidently went on to prove his thesis from myth, but how long he took about it and how he integrated this part with the rest of the poem is not known.[71] The poem is a very clear illustration of how long discourses can be unified by simple, yet logical, devices.

## 'SIMONIDES'

Fr 8 West. Lines 1–11 state the moral advice, and the last couplet directs it to an individual; protasis and apodosis.

SOLON

Fr 4. Lines 1–8 form the introduction: 'The gods will never destroy this city, but the folly of its citizens and leaders will.' This folly is described in 8–14; how it destroys the city, in 15–29. The main point in the latter section is that Justice, when it comes, affects the whole city, and not just the individuals responsible for the crimes. Lines 15–16 are transitional; 17 is a heading; 18–22 list some of the woes encountered (war, stasis); these are summed up by ταῦτα μέν in 22, which serves also to lead into the next point. There follows a slight awkwardness, in that Solon's wish to mention the plight of the poor in particular is somewhat confused by the introduction of an antithesis between ἐν δήμωι (22) and γαῖαν ἐς ἀλλοδαπήν (23). Line 26 closes the ring by echoing 17 (οὕτω clearly has the force of 'QED'); the line also serves as a heading for the next three lines, which at once expand and reinforce the thesis. The poem ends with Solon's advice to follow the course of Εὐνομίη. Lines 1–31 stand in protasis to 32–8.

Fr 13.[72] Lines 1–8 are the germ of the whole. Solon prays for prosperity from the gods; he would not have it unjustly. For (9–10), wealth from the gods is an abiding gift, but wealth earned by unjust means brings punishment from Zeus (11–25). τοιαύτη Ζηνὸς πέλεται τίσις (25) sums up, and leads into further description of the nature of this punishment. It appears sometimes in this, sometimes in later generations. This sentiment echoes πάντως ὕστερον ἦλθε δίκη (8). θνητοὶ δέ (33) opens a new section. Mortals know nothing, and think that all will turn out well; they delight in blind hopes. The argument is inherent in what has preceded; Zeus, not men, commands a larger perspective spanning the generations (25ff); it is therefore to him, and not to hope, that we must look for prosperity (7–13). Two series of examples (37–42 and 43ff) then illustrate the argument of lines 33–6. The second, like the first, shows that men's fortunes are entirely in the hands of the gods, but the emphasis is slightly different. Lines 37–42 speak of afflictions each man hopes he will be spared, while 43ff speak of men's hopes for happiness in their several professions. The structural device used throughout these lines is essentially ἄλλος μέν ... ἄλλος δέ, but with considerable variation in the syntax and amount of time devoted to each instance (χὤστις μέν 37, ἄλλος 39, εἰ δέ τις 41; σπεύδει δ᾽ ἄλλοθεν ἄλλος in 43 is another heading, then ὁ μέν 43, ἄλλος 47, 49, 51, ἄλλον 53, ἄλλοι 57). At line 63 Solon begins a summary section; all the principal notes are sounded again. In the last line, ἄλλοτε ἄλλος ἔχει is perhaps feeble, but it shows that the poet is consciously trying to round off the whole work. Throughout the poem the idea of 'wealth' is never very far away.

πλοῦτος in line 71 is not very much different from ὄλβος in line 3 and identical with χρήματα in line 7. The emphasis of the second section of the poem (9–32) is admittedly different from that of the conclusion (71–6) in that the latter speaks simply of too much wealth whereas the former concentrates on the means by which the wealth is acquired. But these ideas are very closely related to one another; in the situation that forms the ultimate background of the poem, the very real political situation of early sixth-century Athens, the power struggle between different groups had a great deal to do with πλοῦτος. Critics have long recognized the paraenetic intent of the poem. Its mainspring is an argument central to all Greek ethical thought: we are but feeble humans, and awareness of our common humanity carries with it a moral imperative to be concerned for justice. Thus the poem moves easily from the stern lesson on the punishment of the unjust to a commentary on the ignorance of mortals. In the middle part of the poem, which gives a thumbnail sketch of contemporary society, each of the characters is shown striving for ὄλβος in his own way.

The poem does not present a tightly argued thesis, certainly. Yet without performing mental acrobatics we can see the connections between the various parts of the poem, and acknowledge that Solon was aware of them. There is a discernible structure which follows patterns we have seen elsewhere. Parataxis does prevent complete clarity in a discourse of this length; but we do not need syllogisms or Isocratean periods to have some kind of plan.

Fr 24. ἰσόν τοι πλουτέουσιν in line 1 governs two antithetical clauses, ὅτωι κτλ (1–3) and καὶ ὧι κτλ (3–6). ταῦτ᾽ ἄφενος θνητοῖσι sums up the second half of the antithesis and provides a heading for what follows (τὰ γὰρ κτλ).

Fr 27. The poem on the ages of man proceeds regularly with one age per couplet, except that the seventh and eighth ages are collapsed into a single couplet, perhaps for variety, but perhaps also because the poet was unable to think of anything in particular to say about each.

Fr 36. 'Which of the purposes I had in bringing the people together had I not accomplished before I ended?' (1f) asks the poet. The syntax is laboured and reveals that it is not yet up to the concise expression of such involved thought. It allows only so much to be set out as a premise, to be included in the next part by means of an anaphoric pronoun. Mimnermus fr 2.1ff is similar:

ἡμεῖς δ᾽, οἷά τε φύλλα φύει πολυάνθεμος ὥρη
ἔαρος, ὅτ᾽ αἶψ᾽ αὐγῆις αὔξεται ἠελίου,
τοῖς ἴκελοι ...

τοῖς ἴκελοι is thought necessary for clarity.[73]

Solon's accomplishments are given in 3–15,[74] and summed up by ταῦτα μέν in 15, which is answered by θεσμοὺς δέ in 18. His behaviour is contrasted then with that of a foolish and rapacious man (20–5); this man would not have been moderate, and the consequences would have been ruinous. For that reason (τῶν οὕνεκα, 26) Solon chose the course he did. The last couplet is in apodosis with lines 20–5.

## TYRTAEUS

Fr 4. The fragment is a ring (Phoebus in line 1 and again in line 10);[75] in the middle section, the contents of the prophecy are given in a series of apparently dependent infinitives. It is somewhat remarkable that the syntactic subordination is maintained for seven lines. The reason is that Tyrtaeus is quoting the oracle, filling out its hexameters with pentameters;[76] the infinitives, standing for imperatives, are either straight from the original or affect to be such. The syntactic subordination is illusory (not 'they brought home Phoebus' instructions, to rule etc' but 'they brought home Phoebus' instructions: "Rule etc"'); but the structure of the poem remains one of logical dependence.

Fr 11. Lines 1–6 give a general introduction, covering most of the topics (though not all) to be treated later. Then come the reasons why the speaker's advice should be followed: ἴστε γάρ (7), οἳ μὲν γάρ (11) (the second γάρ carries on the first, since what is said in 11ff is not an explanation of anything in 8–10). This takes us to line 20; lines 11–20 contain an antithesis between men who stand firm (11–13) and those who flee (14–20). ἀλλά in 21 starts the new section, which gets down to the details of the fighting; 21ff give advice on how to conduct yourself while the lines are yet apart, 29ff when you come to close quarters;[77] finally, some advice for the γυμνῆτες in 35ff.

The plan of the whole is not especially organic, and the ending in particular is very loose. On the other hand, there is some organization: lines 1–20 follow familiar patterns, and 21–34 move naturally from fighting at a distance to fighting at close quarters. Lines 21ff evolve out of the first section by antithesis with 14–20.

Fr 12. The rhetorical flavour of lines 1–12 has led Wilamowitz, Fränkel, and others to reject the poem as spurious. As Jaeger replied, there is much that is 'rhetorical' in early poetry;[78] indeed, poetry was the source for many of the verbal tricks of the early orators. No one suggests that the conclusion to Solon's poem on Εὐνομίη is spurious, though it fairly bristles with rhetorical devices. The particular device used here to achieve emphasis – repeated negatives – is one which can be illustrated again and again from archaic poetry; this passage simply represents a common tendency taken to an extreme.[79] The 'logic' of the poem is hardly subtle enough to be fifth century, still less Sophistic (so Wilamowitz, *Sappho und Simonides* 257 n 1; cf Fränkel, *Dichtung und Philosophie* 175 n 9).

The poem works along familiar archaic lines. Lines 1–9 stand in protasis to 10–12. Lines 13–20 expand on 10–12; 20 refers back to 10 with a verbal echo. Lines 21f are a transition to the next half of the poem, which in turn has two halves, one on the honours given to the man who dies nobly in battle (23–34), the other on the man who returns victorious and alive (35–42). A couplet containing the exhortation rounds things off. Even a superficial comparison with a later elegy like Theognis 903–28 shows the difference between the ages. And the strict symmetry of the first ten lines can be evidence for an early or a later date (see above pp 75, 77).[80]

Fr 10.  Lines 1–12 are clearly a unit, as are 15–30. The other fragments are organized in sections of roughly this length, but there are no real inner, organic connections between one section and the next. Lines 1–12 could easily go with 15–30 as one poem, either section coming first. The difficulties in the text lie in 13–14 and 31–2. Lines 13–14 fit poorly after 1–12; there is no ἀλλά, δέ, or anaphoric pronoun to mark out the exhortation, as in frr 10.15, 10.31 = 11.21, 11.1, 11.29, 11.35, 12.43, 19.12.[81] West indicates in his apparatus a suspicion that something has dropped out after line 12, and suggests also the possibility that a new poem begins at line 13. But μαχώμεθα in 13 cannot be followed by ὦ νέοι, ἀλλὰ μάχεσθε in 15. Diehl and others begin a new poem at 15 for this reason, and perhaps because ὦ νέοι, ἀλλὰ μάχεσθε looks like a beginning; yet the phrase could indicate a continuation. All these problems disappear if Wassenbergh's solution (Sitzler, *Bursians Jahresberichte* 133 [1907] 123) to place lines 13–14 before line 1 is adopted. The couplet becomes the heading; γάρ in line 1 begins the detailed exposition; περὶ παίδων is picked up in 5f, and ψυχέων μηκέτι φειδόμενοι in 18.

Lines 15ff fall into two antithetical halves after an introduction, one on the disgrace of old men dying in battle, the other on the fineness of young men doing so. We expect an exhortation to end the poem, but the one in 31–32 is weak. Its point is different from that of 15ff (individual courage versus collective courage), and it is suspicious that the couplet recurs in fr 11.21–2. The couplet may safely be deleted.

## XENOPHANES

Fr 1.  Lines 1–12 describe the physical preparations for the next stage of the symposium, 13–24 give advice to the party-goers for their conduct during it. A heading of one couplet may have been lost (note γάρ, line 1).[82]

Fr 2.  (Cf above pp 75, 77.) The poem has two halves: lines 1–12 say that an athlete's prowess is not worth as much as Xenophanes' σοφίη; 13–22 say why. There is probably no significance in the fact that running, the pentathlon, wrestling, boxing, the pankration and horse-racing (1–10) reappear in the order boxing, pentathlon, wrestling, and running (15–17); the sequence is not precisely reversed, and the reason why running is first in 1ff and last in 15ff is that it is πρότιμον (17).

## IBYCUS

PMG 282(a).[83] The loss of the opening stanza(s) is lamentable; there may have been something that anticipated the argument of the last one. Even as the poem stands, it is implausible to view the closing lines on beauty, glory, and song as a feeble addition, provoked by the catalogue which precedes (39ff). Helen, Aphrodite, and Cassandra figure in lines 5, 9, and 11f; words connected with singing, poetry, and fame are found at lines 2, 6, 12, 23ff. The whole of lines 1–45 is in protasis to lines 46–8. τοῖς μέν in 46 sums up only the immediately preceding lines, it is true; but if the poet's intent was clear from the beginning – as it must have been – then his meaning in the closing lines is that Polycrates will enjoy fame not only like the people in 39ff, but like all the heroes. In particular, he will be famous for beauty; thus Troilus and Zeuxippus come last. The 'logical' progression is from 'famous people' to 'people famous for beauty' to 'Polycrates.' In Sappho fr 16, the progression is: 'The most beautiful thing is what one loves; Helen (who is like Anactoria) and her love (which is like mine) prove this; thus I love Anactoria.' Her last statement gains its full significance only when we recognize the relevance of all that has gone before.

Page translates 46f 'among them [πέδα, preposition] for evermore, Polycrates, you too shall have fame for beauty everlasting,' which at least ties 47f to what precedes, but ignores the μέν in 46.[84] Barron translates

'Their beauty is everlasting [πέδα = πέδεστι, with punctuation after 46].[85] And you too, Polycrates, shall have fame for ever.' This recognizes the μέν but not the force of καὶ σύ, which is to imply that Polycrates also has κάλλος. Perhaps no translation can capture both points, but the following may be suggested: 'As they will forever be known for beauty, so you, Polycrates, will have fame for ever, as my song and renown can give it.'

PMG 286, 287. Each poem is divided into two antithetical halves.

### ANACREON

The structure of Anacreon's poetry often reveals a remarkable integration of syntax, metre, and argument. PMG 358 contains one long sentence which falls into two halves, each of which occupies one stanza:

σφαίρηι δηὖτέ με πορφυρῆι
βάλλων χρυσοκόμης Ἔρως
νήνι ποικιλοσαμβάλωι
συμπαίζειν προκαλεῖται·

ἡ δ', ἔστιν γὰρ ἀπ' εὐκτίτου
Λέσβου, τὴν μὲν ἐμὴν κόμην,
λευκὴ γάρ, καταμέμφεται,
πρὸς δ' ἄλλην τινὰ χάσκει.

ἡ δέ in line 5 is a pivot. In PMG 357, also one sentence, five lines are devoted to Dionysus, then three to the poet, and three to Cleoboulus. PMG 388 is constructed around πρὶν μέν (1–9) and νῦν δέ (10–12, protasis and apodosis).[86] PMG 395 falls into two halves, each a stanza long, the first devoted to the poet's old age and the second to Hades. PMG 417, which has three parts, works the same way, and the single stanzas preserved in PMG 360 and 361 are each nicely self-contained (compare also the four iambic dimeters in PMG 427). On the other hand, PMG 347 shows that Anacreon did not keep this up interminably; for variety, the division between two of the stanzas is eliminated (lines 6f). Similarly PMG 346 fr 1.6f. Compare PMG 348, with its structure of three versus five lines; also PMG 357.

### SIMONIDES

PMG 542. Little can be said about this poem's plan. The first stanza may have been a general introduction; the poet then went into detail by returning to the subject of the opening lines at the beginning of the next stanza. The argument ('men cannot be good; their goodness depends on what the gods give them') occupies the second stanza and half the third, and forms a premise to what follows ('so I will blame no man if the evil he has done was not his fault; let a man only have what virtues one can expect'). The incisive gnome in lines 39–40 epitomizes the whole poem. One section grows into the next, but whether the whole was carefully organized cannot be determined without the first stanza.

# 3

# Elegy and the Genres of Archaic Greece

Our study began with words and phrases, and moved on to entire poems; we now come to consider the genres of literature to which the poems belong. The principal aim of this chapter is to explore the origin and nature of archaic elegy. Of course the attempt has been made many times, and with varying results; the evidence is full of pitfalls. However, the recent work of Martin West in his *Studies* has laid the foundation for a more thoroughgoing analysis. There are two points that I particularly wish to stress: first, that the long association of 'elegy' with 'elegiac metre' has confused the discussion; secondly, that the body of verse known as elegy (perhaps with accretions or subtractions) can be defined only by comparing the way other genres are defined.

Let us review the traditional evidence and arguments. In defining genres such as the paean, dithyramb, hyporchema, or skolion, we are assisted to some extent by the Alexandrian classifications, and can deduce some of the generic characteristics from the poetry itself. References in fifth- and fourth-century writers help further. It is different with elegy; the name of the genre, and the metrical definition that goes with it, were artificial inventions of the fifth century. The term ἐλεγεῖον, 'elegiac couplet,' is derived from ἔλεγος, 'lament'; but it cannot be shown that this is of significance for the origin of the whole genre.[1] The difficulty is well known: no archaic poem known to be a dirge is written in elegiac couplets; no archaic poem written in that metre can convincingly be called a dirge.

Admittedly, one or two poems of Archilochus (fr 13, frr 9–11) have been claimed but it is more probable that these are paraenetic elegies in which the death of loved ones also happened to be the occasion for exhortation.[2] In any event, Archilochus and other early authors were already using the metre for a wide variety of purposes, and any original association with the lament that may have existed seems to have been forgotten. If there was such an association at some time in the Dark Ages, we would have to suppose that the memory of it was retained even after the use of the metre was widely extended, and that this knowledge was passed on through the archaic age to the fifth century, when some theorist named the metre; and all this happened without a hint in contemporary evidence. Possible, but not very likely.

This theorist may have been Damon of Athens (cf Plato *Rep.* 3.400b); but whoever he was, it is his predicament that we need to consider. West's observation (*Studies* 7) is very much to the point: what we call elegy – that is, verse in the elegiac metre – was not known before the fifth century by any common name; 'and therefore, conspicuous though it was as a body of verse, it was impossible to name the metre after it.' The term ἐλεγεῖον implies that, somewhere, there were ἔλεγοι in elegiac couplets; what we need to find is an identifiable body of such ἔλεγοι.

One suggestion is that of D.L. Page,[3] that there was a Peloponnesian school known for such compositions, represented for us by Echembrotus of Arcadia and Sacadas of Argos. The former won the prize for aulody at the Pythian Games of 586, and the inscription on the tripod he dedicated is recorded by Pausanias. Echembrotus says that he won singing μέλεα καὶ ἐλέγους (Paus. 10.7.4ff; see West, *Iambi et Elegi* II 62). In the same passage Pausanias, drawing on Pythian victory lists, records the three auletic victories of Sacadas, who according to the pseudo-Plutarch (*De musica* 1134a) was a poet of μέλη τε καὶ ἐλεγεῖα μεμελοποιημένα. We do not know if Echembrotus' ἔλεγοι were written in elegiac couplets, or if Sacadas' ἐλεγεῖα were laments, but it is possible.[4] However, to speak of a 'school' is to be somewhat over-confident with the evidence; a third member has been claimed in Clonas, but he may have been Theban, not Tegean (*De musica* 1133a).[5] It is curious, too, that our theorist should choose an obscure Peloponnesian tradition to provide the name of an Ionic genre, especially when a much more 'conspicuous body of verse,' regularly written in elegiacs in the fifth century, was available in the form of epigrams.

These bits of information from the pseudo-Plutarch and Pausanias do however point us in a promising direction, not to the Peloponnese, but to musical contests, where both Echembrotus and Sacadas made their mark. Plutarch's information about Sacadas is given in support of his contention that aulodes originally sang ἐλεγεῖα μεμελοποιημένα. His other evidence is, significantly, the inscription concerning the musical contests at the Panathenaic Games.[6] The phrase μέλεα καὶ ἔλεγοι, as Echembrotus has it, and which later became μέλη τε καὶ ἐλεγεῖα μεμελοποιημένα, was probably a regular part of the rules for aulody at these contests. Note also the expression of Pausanias, who cites Echembrotus' inscription to support the statement that 'aulody consisted in the singing of the most dismal aulos-songs ($\mu\acute{\epsilon}\lambda\eta$) and $\acute{\epsilon}\lambda\epsilon\gamma\epsilon\hat{\iota}\alpha$ sung to the accompaniment of the aulos.'[7] It is possible that we have here a type of poetry which could have given the metre its name: fairly stylized formal laments sung to the aulos at musical contests. The subject-matter would have been mythological.[8] The original metre was probably not elegiac, but melic, because Echembrotus' inscription is one of the rare genuine epigrams composed in lyric cola, probably the only one from the archaic period.[9] This is remarkable enough in itself, and unbelievable if the competition was for poetry in the elegiac metre. The explanation must be that Echembrotus was a $\mu\epsilon\lambda o\pi o\iota\acute{o}\varsigma$, and composed his victory-inscription in his own idiom. This hypothesis finds confirmation in an epigram to be dated to the first half of the fifth century, AP 13.28;[10] it too has lyric cola, and the epigram is in commemoration of a dithyrambic victory. However, by the fifth century, in time for our theorist, these laments were regularly composed in elegiacs. Presumably they were found at musical contests in locations other than Delphi and Athens. It may be relevant that the pseudo-Plutarch (De musica 1134c) credits a troupe of aulodes including Sacadas with establishing the Gymnopaedia and other Peloponnesian games. We have here not an obscure local genre, but one known across Greece, and therefore 'conspicuous' enough to give the metre its name. We may note also that Pericles reinstituted[11] musical contests at the Panathenaic Games in the 440s; this may have helped bring these $\acute{\epsilon}\lambda\epsilon\gamma o\iota$ to the attention of the theorist, if he was at Athens.

This, then, is the evidence normally adduced for the definition of elegy (with a few addenda). Whatever the reason $\acute{\epsilon}\lambda\epsilon\gamma o\iota$ were chosen for the name of the metre, the naming was almost certainly an artificial expedient, and tells us nothing about the origin of the genre. It could have been strongly doubted in the first place that the metre of a poem alone determined its genre during the archaic period. To be sure, there were broad distinctions which the archaic poet would have recognized, like that between spoken and sung verse (although forms like the elegiac couplet itself, which could be spoken, chanted, or sung, show that this boundary was not absolute).[12] There are typical Ionic, Aeolic, and Doric metres which correspond to certain types of poetry. But the association of specific metres with specific types of poetry is a matter almost of accident. For example, the hexameter was at first virtually the only metre used for epitaphs and metrical inscriptions. In the mid-sixth century, iambics and elegiac couplets made an appearance; but iambics never became popular for the purpose. By the end of the century elegiacs had won the field. After a period of experimentation, therefore, a common practice was somehow adopted.[13] Thus, Archilochus has a wide variety of epodic metres; a century later, Hipponax has noticeably fewer (so far as can be judged from our sources). Even epic has a similar pre-history, although it first appears in hexameters and has that metre throughout antiquity; it is probably correct to regard the hexameter as Ionic normalization of originally freer dactylic rhythms.[14] An individual metre may come to be associated with a genre, and as a result of that association acquire a certain ethos; the ethos is not original with the metre, such that its use in a particular genre is inevitable.

Further evidence that metre alone was not decisive in determining archaic genres can be found. First, the same metre could be put to manifold uses. Hipponax wrote lampoons in hexameters (albeit in parody of epic); the ribald *Margites* had irregularly alternating hexameters and trimeters, as apparently did Xenophanes' *Silloi (Vors.* 21 B 14; cf also Hipponax frr 23, 35.) There were few subjects that could not be expressed in elegiacs. Secondly, and conversely, poems of a similar character and subject could be composed in different metres. Some of Archilochus' tetrameter poems seem to have been martial exhortations like the poems of Tyrtaeus and Callinus, and there is nothing to distinguish Semonides' reflections in fr 1 from many an elegiac poem, save the metre. Moral reflection is not out of place in Archilochus' tetrameters, either (frr 128, 130–4). The subject of Archilochus fr 24 (welcoming a friend from abroad) is similar to that of Theognis 511–22; Anacreon laments a friend in tetrameters (fr iamb 2 West = *PMG* 419); Archilochus writes both elegy (frr 9–11) and iambus (fr 215) on the death of his brother-in-law; Solon expresses his views in elegiacs or iambics indifferently; indeed, the term ἴαμβος includes poems in tetrameters and epodic metres, as well as 'iambics.'

Metre, then, may be at most *one* of the regular features which should be included in a generic definition, along with, say, subject-matter and dialect, as in epic. But we cannot define epic simply as 'a hexameter composition;' no more can we define elegy as 'an elegiac composition.'

If an archaic elegy is not some distant descendant of a lament, and it is not a composition in elegiac couplets, what is it? At present we have no answer, but one available course of action is to see how the other genres are defined. This may suggest some means whereby the mass of verses in the elegiac metre can be called a genre, in an archaic sense.

The poetry of archaic Greece falls easily into two groups, each with fairly clear definitions: epic with its derivatives and lyric genres. The first is defined by what we may call 'literary' characteristics. Epic has its metre, subject-matter, and dialect; it also has a certain style or tone; it has stock episodes, descriptions, and similes; the poet normally remains anonymous behind his verse. The derivatives of epic borrow from it their metre and language, and are further distinguished by their subject-matter or purpose: theogonic, didactic, philosophic, gnomic, and oracular.

As Dover and West have remarked, the most important thing about a lyric genre is the occasion with which it is associated.[15] A skolion is a drinking-song; a paean is (roughly) a song associated with the worship of Apollo; a dithyramb is sung in celebration of Dionysus, an epinician was for an athletic victory, a hymenaios for a wedding, and so on. That some of the genres are named after ritual chants (eg the hymenaios for ὑμὴν ὦ ὑμέναιε) probably supports this view; we may refer also to the simple folk songs of Sappho and others (see the Carmina Popularia in PMG). Parallels from primitive cultures offer further corroboration.[16]

While ordinary occasions of celebration may account for the origin of lyric poetry, however, they do not account for its state of development in archaic Greece. Most of the poems are far more sophisticated than folk songs, and contain extended mythological sections, elaborate literary diction, and an artificial dialect (in 'Doric' and, in so far as they borrow from epic, Ionic genres), even conventional τόποι and structural patterns (in Pindar's epinicians). All these features seem more like the literary characteristics by which the first group of archaic genres is defined. Certainly they reveal the poet's own art, and cannot be explained by reference to the occasion alone.

Indeed, it seems that as poets became more accomplished, and more conscious of their abilities, the lyric genres underwent a sort of evolution by which they were gradually liberated from their occasions. No genre was exempt from this process, even though some developed at a different pace, and older forms continued to exist alongside newer ones (eg devotional and literary dithyrambs). Eventually the poem and its occasion were divorced completely, and we find poets writing works in their studies, to be read by others purely as literature. This 'bookishness' characterizes the Hellenistic period, but it is anticipated by writers like Choerilus and Antimachus.

We may distinguish therefore three stages: (1) purely 'occasional' poetry; (2) poetry with developed literary characteristics, but still connected in some way with an occasion; (3) purely 'bookish' or literary genres. The boundary between the second and third stages is very firmly drawn. Within the second stage, however, there is a spectrum of possibilities, between poetry almost entirely divorced from its occasion and poetry fairly closely tied to it. For example, Alcman's poetry may be placed towards the 'occasional' end of the spectrum, while literary dithyrambs and the longer Homeric Hymns are much closer to the other end. Sappho's wedding-songs belong to the first stage, although the boundary between stages one and two is not always clearly defined.

This scheme is, I think, a faithful representation of the general historical situation. But let us see how matters stand with the individual genres. I should stress that the comments that follow are not meant to provide an exhaustive or definitive discussion of each genre, but merely to test the validity of the scheme. Apart from the basic definition, I give only information relevant to my purpose; further references will be found in the notes.

1   *Paean.*[17] The name comes from cries like ἰή ἰὲ Παιάν, with which a poetic song is associated as soon as we have evidence (*Il.* 1.473). The cry was perhaps originally one for help (Aesch. *Ag.* 146), but its extension to include occasions of thanksgiving for deliverance, good fortune (*Il.* 1.473, 22.391), or occasions of general exuberance (*hAp.* 516ff, Sapph. fr 44.33, Theog. 779) was natural; the god who plagues also heals. The paean was most appropriately addressed to Apollo, but could be directed to Zeus, Artemis, Asclepius, and others.

Pindar's paeans are songs to Apollo on occasions honouring the god. There are calls for help and thanks rendered, as appropriate to the ritual basis of the genre. There are mythological narratives about Apollo, which the form of prayers would lead one to expect. Details about the city and the festival occur naturally. More complex features, shared by other forms of choral poetry, include the use of elaborate poetic language and metre, and the extension of the poem's mythological section. Just how far the myth could be extended is best considered in conjunction with the next genre.

2   *Dithyramb.*[18] Our earliest evidence for the dithyramb (Archil. fr 120) shows it to be a choral song for Dionysus. The Archilochean fragment seems to imply a fairly spontaneous affair, and cries like θρίαμβε διθύραμβε also seem to point to an original stage one. In later times, however, we find Lasos of Hermione, Simonides, Pindar, Bacchylides, and others participating in dithyrambic contests and writing poetry far removed from its origins in worship. The poems are in the main mythological narratives, with little or no reference to Dionysus. The first recorded instance of this type of composition dates to around 600 BC, and is by Arion of Methymna, who Herodotus says (1.23) was the first to write, name, and διδάξαι dithyrambs. διδάξαι means he trained a chorus, and probably implies an elaborate effort; 'naming' implies narratives like those of Bacchylides.

The poetry written for dithyrambic competitions is decidedly stage two, approaching stage three. The relevance of the occasion is marginal; the poems still have to be performed somewhere, but that is all. True religious dithyrambs, some of which survive in Pindar, continued however to exist alongside the literary dithyramb. The development of the latter does not seem to have been a matter of evolution in a strict sense, but occurred somewhat artificially with the introduction of contests. Once dithyrambs appeared in this form, they continued to develop literary features, and as a result of various innovations in the fifth century, their music and language became quite distinctive.

In post-classical times there was occasional uncertainty about the distinction between paeans and dithyrambs. A scholion on Bacchylides 22–3 (ed Snell-Maehler, 128) informs us that Callimachus, noting the occurrence of the ritual cry ἰή, placed poem 23 among the paeans. Aristarchus, however, pointed out that the cry was also found in dithyrambs, where he classified the poem because of its mythological narrative (compare the remarks at ps.-Plut. *De musica* 1134e). Of course, when poem 23 was performed, there was no doubt about its occasion. Yet we should not dismiss the scholars' quarrel as an irrelevant later confusion. Once paeans and dithyrambs were taken out of the context of their original performance and read only in books, there may well have been little to distinguish them. Otherwise, it is hard to see why disagreement arose at all. Aristarchus probably had no better information than Callimachus on the subject; I suspect that the dictum about mythological narratives being peculiar to dithyrambs is overly rigorous, the product of an editor's desire for neat criteria. We may surmise, then, that some paeans did indeed look exactly like literary dithyrambs; that is, they consisted mainly in mythological narrative, with few overtly religious features. Unfortunately no paean of this description survives to clinch the case. Bacchylides 17 may be one; it was performed at Apollo's island Delos, and the myth it relates was relevant to the foundation of the festival (see Snell-Maehler, xlix n 2). There is actually a mention of paeans (129), followed directly by a prayer to Apollo, although that god can be found in dithyrambs too (Bacchyl. 16.10), and the paeans in the poem arise naturally from its narrative. The only real indication that the poem is a dithyramb, however, is that it has been transmitted to us among them. Its placement there may have been an editorial mistake. If, then, Bacchylides 17 is a paean, it is evidence that the genre had developed well into the second stage.

3  *Encomium.*[19] In archaic times the term seems to have been used as the equivalent of 'epinician,' though in theory it could have been applied to any song performed ἐν κώμωι. Consequently, 'encomium' came to have the meaning 'praise of a man,' and a rhetorical genre grew up which had that purpose. In Alexandrian editions, when the term 'skolion' had lost its original meaning, poems which were true skolia were placed among the encomia, for want of a more appropriate category. Because poems sung after dinner might extol a fellow symposiast, it so happens that some skolia found in the Alexandrian books of encomia (or presumed by modern editors to belong there) are encomia in the later sense; but this accident has no bearing

on the practice of archaic times, when 'encomium,' as far as our evidence goes, was not the name of a genre.

4 *Skolion*.[20] A rather general term covering any after-dinner song; indeed, poems originally written for entirely different purposes (for example, poems by Stesichorus) could be performed by a guest as a contribution to the entertainment, and called a skolion. The name comes from the irregular or 'crooked' order in which such pieces were offered during the evening, as opposed to the regular order ἐπὶ δεξιά in which everyone gave their compulsory piece after dinner. Poems written specifically for the symposium usually reflect very closely the conditions of the party and the typical thoughts of the party-goers and belong to the first stage of development of lyric genres, but the artistic efforts of poets like Anacreon illustrate the second stage.

5 *Prosodion*.[21] A poem sung during a procession. Mythic content appears in the short fragments of Pindar's and Bacchylides' prosodia, perhaps implying a later stage of development.

6 *Partheneion*.[22] A poem written for a chorus of girls. Alcman's examples, which are closely concerned with the details of the celebration, have features that point to an earlier stage in the evolution of the genre. There are, however, more complex features as well: the long mythological section; poetic similes; the structural device of using a gnome as a pivot; and (possibly) recurring τόποι.[23]

It is possible that a hidden purpose unites the different parts of Alcman's Partheneion (*PMG* 1). The story of the sons of Hippocoön gives rise to the sentiments of 36ff, which in turn lead to the praises sung of Agido and Hagesichora. The poet advocates the pious pursuit of τὰ πὰρ ποδός, and implies that the present song is precisely that kind of activity.[24] Such a self-consciously philosophical meaning in the poem might qualify as an example of the poet's intervention, even if the values are shared by all; the poet in his wisdom has begun to determine what may be said on an occasion, rather than to accept the demands the occasion imposes (compare further below on epinicians). It is, however, uncertain that this meaning can properly be attributed to the composition.

Pindar's partheneia are of course written in literary Doric; some typically Pindaric sentiments occur in fr 94a. Fr 94b is very closely tied to the circumstances of the performance. These sparse fragments do not give a detailed picture of Pindar's partheneia, but it is likely that they shared the literary characteristics of his other poetry.

7 *Hyporchema*.[25] This is a poem written to accompany a dance. All choral poetry is danced, but in this genre, it seems, the dance is vigorous and assumes first place of importance. Sometimes the editorial task of determin-

ing the genre was helped by references in the poetry to dance movements (cf Pind. fr 107). Such aid was not always available, and if the dance had been performed in honour of Apollo, the poem could just as easily have been included among the paeans; if during a procession, among the prosodia.

In Pindar's hyporchemata there is gnomic and mythological content, but we do not know precisely how this material was integrated into the poems.

8   *Threnos.* Pindar's dirges are professional efforts (examples of the second stage of development), but there is no satisfactory evidence of the poet's personal views, since the thoughts on the afterlife set out in frr 129, 130 and 131a are probably a faithful reflection of the audience's beliefs, and imply nothing about Pindar's own (cf *Ol.* 2 and fr 137).

9   *Hymenaios.*[26] The name comes from the cry ὑμὴν ὦ ὑμέναιε; there was an eponymous mythical figure Hymenaios, as there was a Linos, an Ialemos, and an Adonis. A wedding-song *(Il.* 18.493; [Hes.] *Scut.* 274; Sapph. fr 111.2, 4; Pind. *Pyth.* 3.17; fr 128c 7). How far the hymenaios developed in archaic times is obscured by the difficulty of identifying some of Sappho's poems as examples. Frr 104–17, for instance, show many of the characteristics of folk songs, and illustrate the first stage very well. If fr 44 is a wedding-song, it probably belongs to the second stage. The question whether fr 31 is indeed a wedding-song is bound up with the problem of determining Sappho's own role in the poem.

10   *Hymn.*[27] The derivation and meaning of ὕμνος are unclear. Early usage does not seem to have a sense more specialized than 'celebration;' the word takes specific meaning from its context. Hesiod uses it at *Op.* 657 to describe the composition with which he won at Chalkis, perhaps the *Theogony* (so West); at *Od.* 8.429 ἀοιδῆς is added to ὕμνος to clarify the meaning. One unlikely etymology connects the word with a Sanskrit one meaning 'sew,' and maintains that ἀοιδῆς ὕμνος means 'stitching of song'; ῥαψωιδία is adduced in support[28] (though the derivation of this word is also problematic; it may be connected with ῥάβδος), as well as ὑφάνας ὕμνον in Bacchylides 5.9 f[29] (cf 19.8). A more plausible etymology (Maas') connects the word with ὑμήν (cf λιμήν/λίμνη), but since the root meaning of this word is taken to be 'band' or 'strip,' the original meaning of ὕμνος comes out to be roughly the same.

It is perhaps possible to maintain the connection with ὑμήν and give an account of the original meaning of ὕμνος which better explains the word's later sense of 'praise of a god.' The repetition of a word like ὑμήν or the name of the god is a very old aspect of cult celebrations.[30] The word ὕμνος may have been derived from one such cult word (ὑμήν), and extended to include all others. The word was further extended to apply to the poetry which grew up in connection with rituals; in most cases these songs were praises of the god. Another semantic shift allowed the meaning 'songs of praise' generally, and the word could be used of men in Pindar and other late archaic authors. Finally, ὕμνος came to mean simply 'song,' so that Anacreon (PMG 485) and others (Ar. Av. 210, Eur. IT 179) could use the word even of a dirge. Normally, however, ὕμνος retained its festive associations, so that Plato was generally correct in regarding ὕμνος and θρῆνος as contrasting genres (Leg. 700b; see also Gorgias Vors. 82 B 5b and Isocrates 4.158).

The meaning of the verb ὑμνεῖν 'to repeat over and over' (eg Aesch. Sept. 7, Soph. Aj. 292) may reflect the original meaning of ὕμνος; note also Pindar fr 128c 6:

> ἁ μὲν ἀχέταν Λίνον αἴλινον ὕμνει.

Sappho fr 117B = PLF Inc. Auct. 24 may be relevant, but everything is obscure:

> †νεσσερ† ὑμήναον
> ὦ τὸν Ἀδώνιον.

'Hymn' as a general term for poetry that is sung is not itself the name of a genre, but it is reasonable to suppose that the praises of gods were recognized as a genre by archaic poets.[31] At least these compositions had elaborate characteristics to which the poets adhered.[32] The rhetorician Menander felt able to illustrate his rules for kletic and other hymns by reference to Sappho, Alcman and Anacreon (Rhetores Graeci III 334.28, 333.9 Spengel), Simonides (PMG 615), Bacchylides (fr 1A), and Alcaeus (Rhet. Gr. III 340.15 Sp.).[33] The features of hymn-form, such as the listing of proper epithets, and the narration of a short myth as a guarantee that the god will answer the concluding prayer result from religious concerns. The monopolizing of the poem by the myth is a literary development, and can be illustrated by the larger Homeric hymns, and very possibly by Alcaeus frr 34, 304 LP = Sappho fr 44A Voigt, 307 and 308.[34] Compare also Alcaeus fr 129 and Sappho fr 1, where the prayer-form only provides a framework for the poem.

11  *Iambus*. M. L. West (Studies 22–39) has reconstructed in convincing detail the occasion that was the ἴαμβος. The slander and abuse characteristic of the genre find parallels in Vedic, Celtic, Slavic, Norse, and Eskimo cultures.[35] These parallels cannot provide a comprehensive understanding of Greek iambus. Certain facts, however, like the existence of a suicide story for the victims of both Archilochus and Hipponax, Archilochus' connections with the cults of Demeter and Dionysus, and the existence of a mythical Iambe who performed lewd entertainments and is said also to have hanged

herself, strongly suggest that invective in early Greece was similarly conventionalized.[36] That the ἴαμβος was performed as part of a regular, publicly sanctioned occasion, and that certain of its features were traditional, can be admitted readily. It is less certain that Lycambes was not as real as Cleon, or that for all the exaggeration and adoption of poses there was not a considerable autobiographical element in the poems.

Among the genre's features are erotic narratives, vilification of thinly disguised individuals or universal types, slander of the high and mighty, the adoption of poses by the performer, a grand and swaggering tone, vulgarity and disrespect for public values, and a preoccupation with everyday concerns like food and money. These characteristics may be explained by reference to the occasion, but individual artistry is also evident, for example, in Archilochus, who was able to raise the stylistic level of the form (see Ch 1 p 41).

12 *Citharody and aulody.* A citharode is someone who sings poetry to the cithara, an aulode one who sings to the aulos; each had several distinctive types of tunes which were called νόμοι, 'nomes.' Citharodes sang a distinctive type of poetry perhaps best described as a non-Ionian alternative to epic.[37] Pseudo-Plutarch, *De musica* 1132c (the source is Heraclides Ponticus), asserts that Terpander sang his own verses and those of Homer in contests; this was the practice in the fifth and fourth centuries, but whether it represented the original form of citharody is not certain. Stesichorus, so far as we know, sang only his own compositions, and it seems likely that Terpander did as well. In the early fifth century we know of no great proponent of the art; in this period the proems (collectively ascribed to Terpander, like rhapsodic preludes to Homer) became standardized. It is plausible that the main part of the performance also consisted increasingly in singing others' poems. Whatever the truth of this claim, citharody took on new life in the mid-fifth century, following many leads from the developing dithyramb.

Aulodes, like citharodes, were presumably singers of soli; and we know that one sort of poetry which they sang was elegy (above, p 87f). Yet they also composed μέλη, which seem to have been not solo but choral performances: paeans and hyporchemata and probably dithyrambs *(De musica* 1134c-e). Sacadas (a victor as an aulete, but also a ποιητὴς μελῶν τε καὶ ἐλεγείων) and Clonas trained choruses *(De musica* 1134b); according to a possible emendation in Athenaeus (13.610c), Sacadas wrote an Ἰλίου Πέρσις.[38] A poem with a title composed by an aulode can only have been a dithyramb.[39]

If the early aulodes wrote dithyrambs, there may have been a close association between aulody and citharody, such as we know existed between dithyramb and citharody in the fifth century.[40] Both genres involved heroic narrative; they differed only in the type of musical accompaniment used, and in mode, the one being choral, the other monodic. Both were elaborate 'literary' efforts composed for competitions. The Locrian tradition of poetry includes citharodes in Xanthus,[41] Stesichorus, and Ibycus, and an aulode in the person of Xenocritus.

The close association of the two genres helps explain why Arion, the first composer of literary dithyrambs, was a citharode. He must have won his fame principally in that capacity, but he cannot have written citharodic dithyrambs. The above argument allows us to believe (what is not difficult in itself) that he was also an aulode.

Aulodes seem to have disappeared from the Pythian lists after 586 (see West, *Studies* 5), and it is true that aulody was never as popular as citharody or aulesis.[42] The reason is perhaps that the aulodes' μέλη constituted a duplication of effort. Dithyrambs were being written for their own contests; more were not needed for aulodic contests. Paeans and hyporchemata were to be had in abundance in the normal run of any festival. Citharody, aulesis, and citharisis, on the other hand, each provided unique forms of entertainment.

It will be seen that citharody and aulody do not fit our evolutionary scheme of analysis for the lyric genres. The reason is that citharody, although technically a lyric genre, has many affinities with epic; and aulody – in the sense used here, the aulody of musical contests – is similarly a genre which is literary rather than occasional by nature.

13   *Metrical Epigrams.*[43] Sepulchral, dedicatory, or other inscriptions in verse are among the earliest examples of writing after the Dark Ages. The only metre used in the beginning was the hexameter. Although many early inscriptions merely impart the essential information in a functional way, some authors attempted to give the work an elegance through their use of Homeric expressions. The patterns of phrasing these writers adopted soon became regularized, even though some sought more original forms. On the whole these inscriptions did not become memorable literary productions until the latter part of the sixth century. By that time the elegiac couplet had come to be used almost exclusively. The innovation seems to have been made at Athens during the Peisistratid reign, when the Acropolis was converted from a military to a religious site and the Kerameikos was expanded.[44] These developments brought with them an increase in business for composers of dedicatory and sepulchral inscriptions; at the same time, all the arts were enjoying the patronage of the tyrant. The earliest elegiac inscriptions show a marked increase in artistic merit over their counterparts in other metres. This fact alone shows the influence of other types of elegiac verse on this new

use of the metre. The same influence is evident in the specific stylistic device of addressing the passerby, which presumably derives from the address to the audience everywhere in elegy. None of the earlier inscriptions has this feature. We may therefore discount any suggestion that ἔλεγοι in elegiac metre, which may nor may not have existed at this time (see above), were responsible for the appearance of these elegiac inscriptions in Attica, even if the earliest examples are sepulchral and even if they often do invite the passerby to lament. A strong association of the elegiac metre with ἔλεγοι, if it existed, ought to have produced such inscriptions long before the middle of the sixth century. Yet *one* of the themes of elegiac verse, its reflections on, and its consolations for, the death of loved ones, may have spurred the innovation. The advantages of the elegiac metre in combining stylistic elevation with concision quickly became obvious; the innovation was a success in Athens and spread elsewhere. By the fifth century, as we argued above, it had also affected the composition of ἔλεγοι, which were by then composed in elegiac metre as a part of musical competitions.

Some of the early elegiac epitaphs are justly famous for their poetic quality. The first great poet we hear of engaged in their composition is, however, Simonides; his major efforts in this regard were of course associated with the Persian Wars. The great military events of those years turned epitaph writing into something of an industry. Anonymous efforts, later ascribed to one of the famous poets such as Simonides or Anacreon, have come down to us.

The dedication of an object or the commemoration of the dead are occasions in a sense, and the verse written for them may be regarded as lyric poetry. The development from simple, functional epigrams to more literary ones is particularly clear from our evidence. The final stage, however, in which the epigrams lost all connection with specific, historical occasions, did not occur until post-classical times. Famous epigrams by Simonides and other poets were collected into anthologies towards the end of the fifth century, along with gnomologies, corpora of sympotic elegies, and collections of skolia. These books of inscriptional epigrams provided models for later authors, and by 300 we find a growing number of imitators. Written in a spirit entirely different from that of the original composers, these new compositions were now literary 'epigrams' in which the dedication or epitaph was fictional. As the art of sympotic compositions came to influence these poems, the word 'epigram' was well on its way to losing its association with inscriptions. Indeed, it soon meant any short poem in elegiac metre.

Nevertheless, the development of the literary epigram is anticipated in the classical period. If at first the style of inscribed epigrams was influenced by that of sympotic elegy, there were also a few fifth-century sympotic poems that imitated the style of the inscriptions. Two of these were included in the Hellenistic collection of Simonides. The beginning of one of them is fr 16 West:

σῆμα καταφθιμένοιο Μεγακλέος εὖτ᾽ ἂν ἴδωμαι,
οἰκτίρω σε τάλαν Καλλία, οἷ᾽ ἔπαθες.

This couplet could not have stood on a real tombstone; yet reference to the σῆμα and the verb οἰκτίρω show its stylistic imitation of epitaphs.[45] Very similar is the pair of tetrameters attributed to Anacreon (fr iamb 2 = PMG 419):

ἀλκίμων σ᾽ ὦ ᾽Αριστοκλείδη πρῶτον οἰκτίρω φίλων·
ὤλεσας δ᾽ ἥβην ἀμύνων πατρίδος δουληΐην.

Both of these poems, however, have notable differences from real epitaphs. They were delivered in symposia, presumably, and are therefore expressions of personal feeling. In both, a complex relationship between the poet and the dead is suggested within the brief compass of the traditional form of the epitaph by expressions or devices not original to it. Simonides takes the point of view of one gazing at the tombstone, rather than writing an epitaph in which the tombstone speaks to the viewer. When he says 'whenever I look on this' he creates a very different emotional effect from 'whenever you pass me by'. The same standpoint allows him to bring in a third party, Callias, and to speak of his pity for him. Expecting to mourn Megacles, the audience learns that the true object of sympathy is Callias. Yet in the end we return to Megacles when we are told that Callias is to be pitied 'for his sufferings,' which is to say, for the loss of Megacles. The implicit compliment to the dead man further elicits our pity for him. Mentally gazing on the tombstone all the while, and having our emotions thus manipulated, we are led to contemplate the awful gap that separates the living from the dead. Anacreon's piece is less emotionally complex, but the pathetic expression 'first of my friends' has a similar intent.

The second poem from the Simonidea is this (AP 7.348; Page, Epigrammata Graeca 216f):

πολλὰ πιὼν καὶ πολλὰ φαγὼν καὶ πολλὰ κάκ᾽ εἰπών
ἀνθρώπους κεῖμαι Τιμοκρέων ῾Ρόδιος.

This, too, is obviously not a real epitaph; but its classical date is urged by two considerations: that Timocreon was not a famous poet who attracted

Hellenistic anecdote-mongers; and that in a Hellenistic product one would expect greater imagination in the selection of details – some famous fact about the poet's life, true or invented (like Sophocles' choking on a grape pit, AP 7.20 = Page, *Epigrammata Graeca* 281f, or the standard picture of Anacreon's ways in AP 7.24 and 25 = Page, ibid 342ff). It seems then that this poem is contemporary with Timocreon. It is possible that either Timocreon composed it himself, or that a friend (or enemy) composed it before or after his death; but in either case its humorous or satirical intent is evident. Delivered viva voce with an announcement 'here's what Timocreon's epitaph will be,' the poem would doubtless go over well at a symposium. But in a collection of epigrams (printed last after others by Timocreon?), it would have a somewhat different aspect. The reader would think less of the real author than of his pose as a writer of epitaphs, and might be inspired to write similar poems.[46]

These three poems illustrate how easily the literary development of a genre can lead to a break with the occasion; indeed, the occasion of the third is fictive. The poems are as interesting for their literary qualities as for their performance of the task at hand; and once considered apart from that original occasion – once read in a book after the people involved are dead – they have only literary interest. They lead directly to the epigrams of the Hellenistic period which are wholly literary from the start and therefore aim at ever more sophisticated variations on the original form.

14    *Epinician*. I have left the epinician to the last because it is the most controversial. It is a choral poem sung on the occasion of an athletic victory, and its origins presumably lie in the unassuming, impromptu songs performed immediately after the victory and accompanied by cheers such as τήνελλα καλλίνικε (Archil. fr spur 324). The controversy focuses on precisely the point that has occupied us in this chapter: the relation of poet and occasion. As is well known, the controversy began in 1962, when Elroy Bundy published his two revolutionary essays on Pindar. Bundy set out to correct the more extreme forms of what is generally called 'historical-biographical' criticism,[47] maintaining that everything in an epinician was designed for one purpose, the praise of the victor. He demonstrated that many passages which had previously been taken as irrelevant expression of the poet's own views were in fact conventional devices designed precisely for the purpose of praise. Criticism since 1962 has largely been taken up with testing the validity of Bundy's conclusions. It has become clear that these conventional devices are numerous and complex, and many scholars have given at least qualified support to Bundy; but controversy still continues over many particular passages.[48]

A detailed analysis is beyond the scope of this chapter, but perhaps I may be allowed the following remarks. A distinction must be made between the poet *qua* poet or σοφός and the poet *qua laudator*. The self-consciousness of the poet is a conventional aspect of the epinician; it is a recurring topos that the victory is not complete without the song to celebrate it. The poet knows his worth and does not hesitate to remind his patron of it. This fulfils the function of praise well enough, for the victor gains in stature along with the poet; but can we properly insist that the topos is a function only of the poet *qua laudator*, and not in part also of the poet *qua* poet? It is the *self*-consciousness of the poet which is important; when he says 'you're a good athlete' and then adds 'and I'm just the man to praise you,' the poet is forcefully making his own recognition a part of the genre. A photographer who insisted on being included in the clients' portraits would be behaving similarly. To assert that Pindar's self-consciousness is only a part of the praise is to assert that he himself distinguished clearly between poet *qua* poetically gifted individual and poet *qua laudator* with social obligations, and strove to hide his own biographical self completely in his public *persona*. It is useful to recall that the formal epinician was, as far as our evidence goes, a creation of the late archaic period, when lyric poets were very much in control of what should be said on a given occasion, and charging fat fees for saying it. The distinction between individual and *persona* is scarcely clear when, for example, Pindar chooses to remind his Aeginetan patrons of their relation in myth with his home city of Thebes. That the first person in choral poetry often preserves an ambiguous balance between reference to the poet and reference to the chorus leader further weakens the distinction.[49] Most scholars believe, too, that Pindar was personally committed to the aristocratic ethos that lies behind many of the epinician's τόποι.

Lyric poets gradually felt less constrained by the demands of the occasion, in some cases renouncing them altogether. A complete break never occurred in the epinician genre; we do not find literary epinicians of the old Doric style in the Hellenistic period. Callimachus did compose some epinician poetry in the elegiac metre, but this was an isolated experiment. (On the other hand, the devices of the epinician were perpetuated in prose and verse encomia.) Inasmuch as poetic self-consciousness is characteristic of classical epinician poetry, however, it is part of the same evolutionary development as the other genres. The poet did intrude to an extent upon the poem. To affirm this is not to open the door to 'historical-biographical' criticism; it is merely to soften the dogmatic tenor of Bundy's original position in a way that many scholars now accept.

Even if our argument is not granted for the epinicians, there is no denying the existence of literary dithyrambs, hymns, and, in the Hellenistic period, epigrams, hymenaioi, and other genres. The relevance to our search for a definition of elegy is this: is there any way we can call the body of elegiac verse a lyric genre as we now understand that term? The answer must be no. Elegy is not defined by its occasion, since there was no single occasion with which it was associated. In fact elegy could be performed on many occasions (see the list in West, *Studies* 10ff), among which there does not seem to be any obvious unity. One might argue that at the beginning of the archaic period it had already undergone the same liberation from the occasion that was eventually characteristic of the other genres. Yet it seems odd that elegy was so far in advance of the others. Moreover, it is hard to see elegy as the end product of the same evolutionary process that produced, for example, the literary dithyramb out of its liturgical ancestor. The elegiac corpus is too varied; and we can hardly posit a single type of poetry as the begetter, whether laments or something else.

Nor does elegy belong with the derivatives of epic, although it is sometimes called that. The metre derives from the epic metre, but we have seen that that is not sufficient in itself to define the genre. At any rate the need for a metre is prior to its existence; a metre is not invented and then sent looking for uses. Elegy does not belong with the epic derivatives because it has no single purpose or subject-matter, and cannot be defined by a combination of 'literary' characteristics.

We are forced to conclude that elegy was not an archaic genre, in any identifiable sense of the word. Is it then a group of genres? It might be possible to divide the corpus according to the various occasions for which the poems were written, and call these genres: sympotic poetry, martial exhortations, political exhortation at public meetings, ἔλεγοι, poems for the κῶμος, etc. This would have some merit; Tyrtaeus at least seems to have been copying a particular type of verse, of which poems by Callinus and probably one by Mimnermus (fr 14) are examples. But if the corpus is otherwise too varied to unite into a single genre, it is too cohesive to permit such fragmentation. The poems of Tyrtaeus and the second book of Theognis, for all their differences, do have something in common beyond their metre and the occasional epicism.

Even if we cannot call elegy a 'genre,' this common character is significant. It can be described in part in stylistic terms: clarity; a fondness of certain figures of speech, notably verbal and logical antithesis and parallelism; the expression of opinions in the form of general propositions, which are then argued in a dialectical spirit by means of a series of illustrations; and a noticeable striving for an 'epigrammatic' style (encouraged by the form). We often find an elevated tone, a fondness of gnomic or paraenetic content, and a dispassionate, reasonable stance on the part of the speaker. None of these characteristics is always present; indeed, their opposites sometimes are.

None is sufficient to define a genre, nor are all of them sufficient together; most are found, in fact, in Homer and Hesiod. Still, by observing these features we are on a promising track. If we had to state their common denominator, I think we should say 'Ionicism.'

If we can say nothing else about elegy, we can say that it was an Ionic form. Indeed, we could say that all Ionic verse is elegy that is not epic or ἴαμβος. As a *classification* of verse we can place it on a par with Doric choral lyric and Aeolic monody. Each of these has features which readily contrast with those just listed for elegy, and neither can be defined as a genre in the strict sense. Elegy is merely something an Ionian composed on occasions when he had something to say in poetry. However, especially in the wake of Ionic epic, it could be exported abroad and imitated by non-Ionians such as Tyrtaeus and Theognis.[50] Aeolic monody was as versatile as elegy, but very much a local product, and Doric poetry was tied to specific occasions. The elegiac couplet was an excellent catch-all metre, especially because of the ease with which it accommodated the elevated language of epic. The metre also offered formal neatness. Originally, iambic and trochaic metres were also used for various informal occasions; like the elegiac couplet, they could be spoken, and required no special musical attainments. We are free to consider Archiloc- hus' reflective tetrameters, Solon's political iambics, and Semonides' verses addressed to a boy on the ephemeral status of mankind (fr 1) in the same category as elegy, where they really have a much better claim to belong than with the obscene lampoons of Hipponax. Eventually, however, the elegiac couplet gained a complete monopoly, as it did for epigrams; but Anacreon could still use trochees for 'elegiac' purposes.

'Elegy' in archaic times, then, cannot be said to refer to a poem in elegiac couplets; nor can the corpus of elegiac verse be called a genre in the same sense that epic, paean or dithyramb can. Nevertheless, with the addition of a fair number of poems in other metres, it can be recognized as a body of verse. The classification is not mere pigeon-holing, but corresponds to something real, as the parallels with Doric and Aeolic verse show. No name readily suggests itself; 'Ionic occasional verse' does not seem specific enough, but 'Ionic monody' lays too much stress on singing, and would include Anacreon's lyric skolia. We shall have to keep calling it 'elegy,' even though the metrical definition implied by this term is inaccurate. It is a conclusion which need not disturb editors, who naturally will continue to arrange their editions along metrical lines; but historians of literature may like to take note of it.[51]

# NOTES

1 Throughout this work the expression 'Greek lyric poetry' refers to the non-epic and non-dramatic poetry of the archaic and classical periods.

2 I give the principal works here. The inaugural essay was by Hermann Fränkel: 'Eine Stileigenheit der frühgriechischen Literatur' *Gött. Nachr.* (1924) 63–127 = *Wege und Formen* 40–96; see further *Dichtung und Philosophie* and other essays in *Wege und Formen*. By Bruno Snell: *Aischylos und das Handeln im Drama* Philol. Suppl. 20.1 (1928) (*Habilitationsschrift* Hamburg 1925); *Die Entdeckung des Geistes* (1946, ⁵1980), tr T.G. Rosenmeyer *The Discovery of the Mind: The Greek Origins of European Thought* (1953); *Poetry and Society* (1961, German tr 1965); *Tyrtaios und die Sprache des Epos* Hypomnemata 22 (1969); *Der Weg zum Denken und zur Wahrheit* Hypomnemata 57 (1978); various essays and the *Gesammelte Schriften* (1966). By Werner Jaeger: *Paideia* I (1934, ²1935, tr by G. Highet, ⁴1954); and the papers collected in *Scripta Minora* (1960). By Max Treu: editions of Sappho (1954, ⁴1968), Archilochus (1959), Alcaeus (²1963); *Von Homer zur Lyrik* Zetemata 12 (1955; ²1968); and other essays.

3 E. Wolff, *Gnomon* (1929) 386–400; O. Seel, 'Zur Vorgeschichte des Gewissen-Begriffes im altgriechischen Denken' in *Festschrift Franz Dornseiff* ed H. Kusch (1953) 291–319; H. Gundert's review of Fränkel's *Dichtung und Philosophie* in *Gnomon* 27 (1955) 465–83; A. Lesky, 'Göttliche und menschliche Motivation im homerischen Epos' *Sitz. Heidelb.* (1961) Abh. 4 1–52 (see further his references at p 1 n 4); Hugh Lloyd-Jones, *The Justice of Zeus* (²1983) and *Females of the Species* (1975) 12, 24, 29ff; M. Dickie, *ICS* 1 (1976) 7–14; W. Rösler, *Dichter und Gruppe* (1980) 14ff; C.J. Rowe, ' "Archaic Thought" in Hesiod' *JHS* 103 (1983) 124–35; M. Griffith, 'Personali-

ty in Hesiod' *ClAnt* 2 (1983) 37–65, with further references; J. Latacz, 'Das Menschenbild Homers' *Gymnasium* 91 (1984) 15–39. See also the brief remarks of K.J. Dover, *JHS* 77 (1957) 322f and *CR* ns 10 (1960) 12; M.L. West, *CR* ns 15 (1965) 159, 222; J.A. Russo, *GRBS* 15 (1974) 139ff; G.S. Kirk in M. Ayrton, *Archilochus* (1977) 41.

4 This word, which corresponds most closely but nonetheless loosely to the English 'history of ideas,' is often used as a label for the views of the Fränkel-Snell school; one hears the phrase 'the *Geistesgeschichte* writers.' We all know to whom this refers, but the designation, though convenient, is inaccurate; nearly all classical scholars have written *Geistesgeschichte*, in the proper sense of the term.

5 *Homer on Life and Death* (1980) ch 2

6 That a metaphorical way of speaking was once non-metaphorical is only an *a priori* assumption; corroboration in the thinking habits of primitive peoples will not be found unless the long discredited theories of Lévy-Bruhl are revived.

7 This concept is excellently explained by Lesky, 'Göttliche und menschliche Motivation', who effectively refutes Snell's views on the notion of 'will' in Homer, though Snell does offer a rebuttal *(Gesammelte Schriften* 55–61). In the 'Afterword' to *Die Entdeckung des Geistes*[5] 283ff and 60 n 2 of the *Gesammelte Schriften*, Snell refers to the 1933 Hamburg dissertation of Christian Voigt, *Überlegung und Entscheidung. Studien zur Selbstauffassung des Menschen bei Homer* (repr as Beitr. zur klass. Philol. 48 hrsg. v. R. Merkelbach [1971]), which he says shows that scenes cited by Lloyd-Jones and Lesky (in his history of Greek literature) as examples of true decisions are nothing of the kind. Voigt's principal argument is that Homer's regular way of reporting a decision, 'It seemed to him better,' reflects no real 'subjective' decision, rather one of two 'objective' alternatives striking the passive individual from without. The choice just happens to you; therefore you have not chosen. However, 'it seems to me better' really means 'I decide' in any language, and in any event the expression presupposes the prior existence of a first person subject, 'me.' Voigt's argument places an unnatural interpretation on the evidence in order to support a given theory and may be fairly accused of special pleading. The weakness of Voigt's thesis is particularly evident in his discussion of the key passage *Il.* 11.404ff; his interpretation is very forced. E. Wolff, *Gnomon* (1929) 386ff, had placed due stress on the key word οἶδα, which Snell glided over in his rebuttal at *Philol.* 85 (1930) 141ff. See also G. Petersmann's trenchant remarks in 'Die Entscheidungsmonologe in den homerischen Epen' *GB* 2 (1974) 147–69.

8 If one wished to answer the argument on its own terms, one could point out that, strictly, Achilles' ultimate action – the withdrawal of his services – forms no part of Athena's advice to him. It is his own idea.

9 So Voigt, *Überlegung und Entscheidung* 82ff.

10 M.L. West, *Hesiod: Theogony* (1966) 40ff; W. Burkert, 'Das hunderttorige Theben' *ws* nF 10 (1976) 5–21; E. Heitsch, *Gött. Anz.* 220 (1968) 180. For the opposing view see A. Heubeck, *Schrift* Archaeologia Homerica Band III, Kapitel x, (1979) 109–16 and *Gymnasium* 89 (1982) 443. More recently, in *The Greek Renaissance of the Eighth Century B.C: Tradition and Innovation* ed R. Hägg (1983), Burkert seems to have tacitly abandoned his dating.

11 See below pp 20ff.

12 Apart from the poems which eventually constituted the Cycle, local epics, theogonies, and oracles are among the sorts of formulaic compositions which were available to the poets.

13 For a similar judgment in the field of early archaic art, and Homer's influence on it, see A.M. Snodgrass, 'Poet and Painter in Eighth-century Greece' *PCPS* ns 25 (1979) 118–30.

14 See in general R. Schmitt, *Dichtung und Dichtersprache in indogermanischer Zeit* (1967) *passim*, but especially ch 9 and Epilegomena; for some useful general observations and warnings, see W. Meid, *Dichter und Dichtkunst in indogermanischer Zeit* Innsbrucker Beiträge zur Sprachwissenschaft Vorträge 20 (1978).

15 'The Poetry of Archilochos' *Archiloque* 183–212

16 Ibid 164

17 Ibid 165. Cf below n 49.

18 'Die Sprachform der altionischen und altattischen Lyrik' *Bezzenbergers Beiträge* 11 (1886) 242–72, 13 (1888) 172–221, 14 (1888) 252–66; 'Zur ionischen Mundart und Dichtersprache' *Neue Jahrb.* 1 (1898) 501–13.

19 Cf Thumb-Scherer, *Handb. d. gr. Dialekte* 231ff, with further references.

20 This is a large problem and I can cite only a selection of the literature. For Homer and Hesiod see J.A. Notopoulos, 'Homer, Hesiod and the Achaean Heritage of Oral Poetry' *Hesp.* 29 (1960) 177–97; C.O. Pavese, *Tradizioni e generi poetici della Grecia arcaica* (1972). For criticism of these views see A. Hoekstra, *Homeric Modifications of Formulaic Prototypes* (1965, repr 1969) 25f; G.P. Edwards, *The Language of Hesiod in its Traditional Context* (1971) 201ff; H. Troxler, *Sprache und Wortschatz Hesiods* (1964) 238; R. Janko, *Homer, Hesiod and the Hymns* (1981) 12f, 84f. That Homer's tradition (irrespective of Hesiod's relation to it) goes back to the Mycenaean mainland without break has been questioned by G.S. Kirk, 'Dark Age and Oral Poet' *PCPS* ns 7 (1961) 34–48 = *Homer and the Oral Tradition* (1976) 19–39; id, 'Objective Dating Criteria in Homer' *MH* 17 (1960) 189–205; id, *The Songs of Homer* (1962) 105ff; for the opposite view see eg D.L. Page, *History and the Homeric Iliad* (1959); G.C. Horrocks, 'The Antiquity of the Greek Epic Tradition: Some New Evidence' *PCPS* ns 26 (1980) 1–11; C.O. Pavese, 'L'origine micenea della tradizione epica rapsodica' *Studi micenei ed egeo-*

*anatolici* 21 (1980) 341–52; A. Hoekstra, *Epic Verse Before Homer: Three Studies* (1981); D.G. Miller, *Homer and the Ionic Epic Tradition: Some Phonic and Phonological Evidence Against an Aeolic 'Phase'* Innsbrucker Beiträge zur Sprachwissenschaft 38 (1982). On the relation of lyric to the Homeric and Hesiodic traditions see C.O. Pavese, *Tradizioni e generi*; B. Gentili, 'Lirica greca arcaica e tarda arcaica' in *Introduzione allo studio della cultura classica* ed F. della Corte I (1972) 59ff; A.M. Bowie, *The Poetic Dialect of Sappho and Alcaeus* (1981). Some scholars have attempted to use the affinity of Greek and Vedic metres to throw light on the early history of lyric and epic: see eg M.L. West, 'Greek Poetry 2000–700 B.C.' *CQ* ns 23 (1973) 179–92 and 'Indo-European Metre' *Glotta* 51 (1973) 161–87; G. Nagy, *Comparative Studies in Greek and Indic Metre* (1974); for damaging criticism of these attempts see A. Hoekstra, *Epic Verse Before Homer* ch 2 and K. Itsumi, *CQ* ns 32 (1982) 59–74. The present study adopts the position that the Dark Ages saw fundamental changes, including the creation of the lyric genres *as we know them*. While certain matters of content such as the themes of praise and blame were passed on in continuous tradition, the first step toward a high literary style for the elegists and iambographers was taken under the influence of epic.

21 See G.P. Edwards, H. Troxler, and R. Janko, cited in the preceding note.

22 On Tyrtaeus see Dover in *Archiloque* 190ff; for elegy see further below Ch 3 n 50.

23 This is the view of the followers of Parry; it has been challenged by M.W.M. Pope, *Acta Classica* 6 (1963) 7ff.

24 Cf Wilamowitz, *Textgeschichte der griechischen Lyriker* Gött. Abh. 4.3 (1900); also published separately (1900) 117.

25 In addition to the argument from comparative material (above, p 9), one might contend that the genres of elegy and iambus, their character and conventions, are fully developed and distinct in Archilochus, and that this points to a pre-existing tradition. To this it could be replied either that the genres are *not* distinct in Archilochus (so Dover in *Archiloque* 183ff), or that in the history of Greek literature all the genres seem to have matured very quickly, in most cases in fact to have sprung to life fully formed (cf on the metres A.M. Dale, *CQ* 44 [1950] 143f = *Collected Papers* [1969] 51f; *CQ* ns 13 [1963] 49f = *Collected Papers* 178f). Cf below Ch 3 n 51.

26 Also, of course, using a closely related metre; perhaps the adoption of the language and the invention of the metre are connected.

27 Cf 'Homeric Epithets in Greek Lyric Poetry' *CQ* ns 7 (1957) 206–23, hereafter referred to as 'Harvey.'

28 With one newly discovered exception, the earliest pieces of writing after the Dark Ages belong to the third quarter of the eighth century; for a Naxian

sherd dating to c 770 see *BCH* 106 (1982) 605 with fig 132. Before 700 we really have only scattered evidence suggesting the hesitant adoption of a new art. It is significant that one of the oldest pieces (the Dipylon oinochoe) is a perfect hexameter. See L.H. Jeffery, *The Local Scripts of Archaic Greece* (1961) 68ff; id in *CAH*² 3.1.819ff; Hansen no 432.

29 R. Finnegan, *Oral Poetry* (1977) 134ff; the shorter poems are all popular ballads. Note also that the wording of these songs suffers many changes, although popular memory is tenacious in respect of plots and motifs.

30 Cf Fr 141 ~Ar. *Vesp.* 1232ff; W. Rösler, *Dichter und Gruppe* (1980) 95ff.

31 *The Justice of Zeus* (²1983) xi

32 ' ... die Denker waren Menschen von Fleisch und Blut mit inneren Widersprüchen, wie wir Menschen sie alle haben, auch mit Liebe und Hass. Die Dichter sind das auch gewesen und auch sie werden heute in eine « Entwicklungsreihe gepresst ». Wenn das Historismus ist, daß man die Menschen als Individuen in ihrer Zeit fassen will, so bekenne ich mich zu der angeblich victa causa.' So Wilamowitz to Julius Stenzel on 26 February 1931: W.M. Calder III, *A&A* 25 (1979) 96. The direction of events seems predictable in hindsight. New interest in style and inner form naturally tended to exclude the historical (cf Snell in *Der Weg zum Denken und zur Wahrheit* Hypomnemata 57 [1978] 105–21; also P. Friedländer, ed Calder, in *A&A* 26 [1980] 90–102); but the two lines of inquiry are not incompatible. – Wilamowitz's remarks on Homeric characterization at *Der Glaube der Hellenen* I (1931, ²1955) 344ff are significant.

33 'Archilochus and the Oral Tradition' in *Archiloque* 119–63

34 J.A. Notopoulos, 'Archilochos the Aoidos' *TAPA* 97 (1966) 311–15

35 G.S. Kirk, 'Formular Language and Oral Quality' *YClS* 20 (1966) 155–74 = *Homer and the Oral Tradition* (1976) 183–200; Albrecht Dihle, *Homer-Probleme* (1970) 49 n 6.

36 Using this procedure, one might have a better chance of proving Tyrtaeus an oral poet than Archilochus, since there are probably more phrases in the former that have exact parallels in Homer (ie are repeated in the same form in the same part of the verse). As far as evidence for systems is concerned, the violation of economy in Tyrtaeus fr 12 may be noted: line 27 ὁμῶς νέοι ἠδὲ γέροντες; line 37 ὁμῶς νέοι ἠδὲ παλαιοί. But the variant could be explained as a corruption in an early stage of the poem's transmission.

37 *Homer-Probleme* 51 n 6

38 In fr 8.1 πολιῆς ἁλὸς ἐν πελάγεσσι, πολιῆς ἁλός and ἁλὸς ἐν πελάγεσσι are both attested in the same part of the verse; the two go together to make an 'adapted' formula. Cf below p 18.

39 To be fair, a strict definition cannot be right; systems do exist. The questions

are, how they should be defined, how they aid improvisation, and whether, even with this broader understanding of formularity, Homer's orality can be proven. I give below in crude outline Lord's and Hainsworth's conceptions of the formula-system; Parry's original theory is different again, but not directly relevant here.

40 For the proponents of the structural formula see J.B. Hainsworth, *Homer* Greece and Rome New Surveys in the Classics 3 (1969) 19 n 2.

41 Ibid 20; see also Hainsworth's *The Flexibility of the Homeric Formula* (1968) 16ff. Lord also objects to the extreme structuralist position in *Harv. Stud.* 72 (1967) 15.

42 One of Page's arguments for Archilochus' orality is the supposed lack of writing material. No one denies that the spread of literacy was made easier by access to large quantities of papyrus through Naucratis in the second half of the seventh century; but that is hardly the point. We need only find something for Archilochus to write on, and almost anything will do: wood, wax, leather (Hdt. 5.58), or even the occasional piece of papyrus, if, as the name βύβλος may suggest (F. Dornseiff, *Hermes* 74 [1939] 209f = *Antike und alter Orient* [²1959] 31f; M.L. West, *Hesiod: Theogony* [1966] 48 n 2; L.H. Jeffery, *The Local Scripts of Archaic Greece* [1961] 56), the Greeks acquired the material through Phoenicia before establishing direct contact with the source. The problem of writing materials is really no problem at all, as J. Pouilloux remarks in *Archiloque* 171. Cf in general Jeffery 50ff.

43 Special problems attend the study of the formulaic use of individual words. Often their recurrence in the same part of the verse is of no significance; but it is clear on the other hand that single words can become localized in one part of the verse (see E.G. O'Neill, *YClS* 8 [1942] 103ff). Single words are not counted as formulae here; but see below n 49.

44 For non-dactylic epodic lines and iambic poems there is of course no criterion by which an 'adapted formula' can be discovered.

45 Hainsworth, *The Flexibility of the Homeric Formula* 99f, 102 n 1. The phrase ἀλλὰ τάχιστα does, however, have some claim to being a formula; see below n 49.

46 In this particular case, of course, the tmesis may impart an epic flavour to the phrase; but this has nothing to do with its being a formula.

47 There have been numerous studies of parallels in diction and subject-matter between Archilochus and the other lyric poets, and the epic. The principal ones are listed here for convenience, and will be referred to by author's name only: J.G. Renner, 'Über das Formelwesen im griechischen Epos und epische Reminiscenzen in der älteren griechischen Elegie' *Einladungsschrift des Freiberger Gymn.* (1871; repr as a monograph 1872); R. Kuellenberg, 'De imitatione Theognidea' (diss, Strasbourg 1877); O. Laeger, 'De veterum epic-

orum studio in Archilochi, Simonidis, Solonis, Hipponactis reliquiis con-
spicuo' (diss, Halle 1885); F. Weigel, 'Quaestiones de vetustiorum poetarum
elegiacorum Graecorum sermone ad syntaxim, copiam, vim verborum per-
tinentes' (diss, Wien 1891); U. Bahntje, 'Quaestiones Archilocheae' (diss, Göttingen 1900) 45ff, for single words only; N. Riedy, *Solonis elocutio qua-
tenus pendeat ab exemplo Homeri* Progr. des Königl. Wilhelms-Gymn. in
München (1902–03) I (1903), II (1904); H. Schultz, 'De elocutionis Pindar-
icae colore epico' (diss, Göttingen 1905); D. Mülder, *Homer und die altjoni-
sche Elegie* Beilage zum Progr. des Königl. Gymn. Andreanum (1906), who
cites parallels in passing; A. Monti, *De Archilochi elocutione* (1907), and his
*Index Archilocheus cum Homerico, Hesiodeo et Herodoteo comparatus*
(1903), *non vidi*; H. Buss, *De Bacchylide Homeri imitatore* (1913); V. Steffen,
'De Archilocho quasi naturali Hesiodi imitatore' *Eos* 46 (1952–3) 33–48; O.
von Weber, 'Die Beziehungen zwischen Homer und den älteren griechischen
Lyrikern' (diss, Bonn 1955); I. Kazik-Zawadzka, *De Sapphicae Alcaicaeque
elocutionis colore epico* (1958). Parallels are noted in the apparatus in many
editions, particularly Tarditi's of Archilochus; Gentili's of Anacreon; Voigt's
of Sappho and Alcaeus; Prato's of Tyrtaeus; Young's of Theognis; Diehl's
*Anthologia Lyrica Graeca*; G. Perrotta and B. Gentili, *Poesia greca arcaica*
(1965); F. Adrados, *Líricos griegos I: Elegiacos y yambógrafos arcaicos* (1976);
C. Prato and B. Gentili, *Poetae Elegiaci: Testimonia et Fragmenta, Pars I*
Teubner edition (1979); see also P. Giannini, 'Espressioni formulari nell' elegia
arcaica' *QUCC* 16 (1973) 7–78; C.O. Pavese, *Tradizioni e generi poetici della
Grecia arcaica* (1972) 154ff; B. Gentili, in *L'Epigramme grecque*, Fondation
Hardt 14 (1968) 69ff; and Page in *Archiloque.*

48 *PKöln* III 126; first published by L. Koenen and R. Merkelbach, 'Apollodoros
(περὶ θεῶν), Epicharm und die Meropis' in *Collectanea Papyrologica:
Texts Published in Honor of H.C. Youtie* I (1976) 3–26.

49 See above p 14. I include here the phrase πολιῆς ἁλὸς ἐν πελάγεσσι. If the
phrase θανάτου τέλος in fr 5.3 is considered a false reading (out of generos-
ity, it has been counted in the percentages in the table), the amount of 'formular' language in the hexameters drops to 11%; in elegy the figure remains at
7%.

All of these percentages naturally do not reveal the total amount of epic
diction in Archilochus, only of epic phrases. To use individual words to
prove oral composition would raise further problems, and probably would not
be successful. Words and word-groups in Archilochus which conform to
clear localizing tendencies in Homer are ἀλλ᾽ ἄγε (4.6), ἐρρέτω (5.4), εὔπλο-
κάμου (8.1), ἀμφεπονήθη (9.11), κλαίων (11.1) ὦ φίλ᾽ (13.6), ἀλλὰ τάχιστα (13.9), μάχηται (15). If these are counted and the phrases in parentheses
excluded, 33% of the language of elegy is formular and formulaic; if the

parenthetical phrases are included, the figure is 38%. Words and word-groups for which the evidence in Homer is insufficient or ambivalent are παρὰ θάμνωι (5.1), κάλλιστον (5.2), ἰήσομαι (11.1), τερπωλάς (11.2), ἐξαῦτις (13.9), ἐπαμείψεται (13.9), and δίδωσιν (16). If all these words as well as the phrases in parentheses are included in the reckoning, and the authenticity of frr 15–17 denied, a figure of 45% formular and formulaic is obtained. The figure might be called respectable, but few scholars will allow all the premises entailed; and it still includes an excessive formulaic component. Note that many of the words common to Archilochus and Homer and cited by Page in support of his contention were part of everyday Ionic: τανύω, σφεν-δόνη, ἀπωθέω, ἔρρω, ἔγκειμαι; or for all we know could have been: ἐκσαόω, ἀμφιπονέομαι, ἐπαμείβομαι, αἱματόεις.

50 See further below pp 40ff.

51 I do not claim to discuss every passage in ancient lyric that has ever been called an imitation, but these are the important or illustrative ones.

52 R. Pfeiffer, 'Gottheit und Individuum in der frühgriechischen Lyrik' *Philol.* 84 (1929) 137–52 = *Ausgewählte Schriften* (1960) 42–54, thinks that the Archilochean and other lyric fragments show a new importance of τλημοσύνη in men's lives. The emphasis is different, but whether it is new rather than generic is not clear.

53 *Gnomon* 45 (1973) 738 n 1

54 In frr 10.15, 11.11, and 11.38, however, the exhortation is to stand close by one's friends; fr 19.13 may refer either to friends or enemies.

55 For example, see Jaeger, *Paideia* I (²1935) 173 (= tr Highet [⁴1954] 125); H.D. Rankin, *Archilochus of Paros* (1977) 41.

56 For significant parallels in Near Eastern literature see A. Lesky, *Sitz. Heidelb.* (1961) Abh. 4 9f. With the passages discussed here compare also Theog. 695f. On self-address see further F. Leo, *Der Monolog im Drama* (1908) 94ff; for the device in tragedy, see W. Schadewaldt, *Monolog und Selbstgespräch* (1926), esp 35ff.

57 The parallels are mentioned in several of the works cited above, n 47. D.E. Gerber, *Euterpe* (1970) 41 cites also *Il.* 3.442 ἔρως φρένας ἀμφικάλυψεν; Harvey (214) thinks *Il.* 11.115 ἁπαλόν τέ σφ' ἦτορ ἀπηύρα is the model for line 3. For literary or psychological subtleties in the poem, see Harvey; M.S. Silk, *Interaction in Poetic Imagery* (1974) 131f; T.B.L. Webster, *Greek Art and Literature 750–530 B.C.* (1959) 31; G.M. Kirkwood, *Early Greek Monody* (1974) 42. Snell's observations on this poem in *Die Entdeckung des Geistes*⁵ 63 (tr Rosenmeyer 52) are typical.

58 κλέψαι νόον is a perfectly normal phrase: *Il.* 1.132, Hes. *Th.* 613, Semon. fr 42 W = *PMG* 525.

59 Anac. *PMG* 358.1, 376.1, 400.1, 413, 428, Sapph. fr 1.15ff; compare further
   Alcm. *PMG* 59(a) 1, Ibyc. *PMG* 287.1, Sapph. fr 130.1.
60 A plausible interpretation of Theog. 949–54 is that the lines are erotic; if so,
   they illustrate the same character. For the paradoxes there cf Anac. *PMG* 428
   ἐρέω τε δηὖτε κοὖκ ἐρέω / καὶ μαίνομαι κοὖ μαίνομαι.
61 Cf below p 40.
62 Accepting Jacobs' join
63 E. Bethe, *Homer* II (1922) 300 n 11, thinks that it is.
64 Von Weber (8ff) argues that the third line shows a 'new' development (increased awareness of experience), and that therefore Archilochus is imitating Homer. In the writing of intellectual history, what is new and old forms
   part of one's conclusions; to use what is thought *a priori* to be new and old
   as an argument for dating is a crude *petitio*.
65 According to Eustratius (on Arist. *Eth. Nic.* 6.7 = Archil. fr 303), Archilochus
   said that Homer composed the *Margites*. This may be a mere inference
   from the 'quotation' of 'Homer's' line by Archilochus (so West in his apparatus; cf also J.A. Davison, *Eranos* 53 [1955] 134ff = *From Archilochus to
   Pindar* [1968] 79ff).
66 For Archilochus it is attested in frr 286–9, and fr (dubium) 305.
67 F. Bossi, *MCr* 8–9 (1973–4) 14f; J. Henderson, *Arethusa* 9 (1976) 165ff; J. van
   Sickle, *QUCC* 20 (1975) 127ff.
68 *ZPE* 37 (1980) 197
69 'Die Elegie des Kallinos' *Hermes* 107 (1979) 385–9
70 A. Debrunner, *Griechische Wortbildungslehre* (1917) 32 (§62). Euripides offers Δυσελένα (*Or.* 1388, *IA* 1316).
71 The white head and chin of the old man in both passages could easily be
   coincidental.
72 That Tyrtaeus loses his grip on the syntax is no indication that his passage is
   secondary; anacoloutha are not at all unusual in this period (note the way
   τοὺς γεραιούς is tacked on in line 20). Dover, in *Archiloque* 190f, argues that
   the inconcinnity of νέοισι followed by ἔχηι in 27f could have been avoided
   if Tyrtaeus had been willing to say νέωι δέ τε like Homer; but this inconcinnity like any other could have been entirely of the poet's own making, rather
   than resulting from the pressure of an awkward original. (Dover takes no stand
   on Tyrtaeus' relationship to Homer, but accepts that some hexameter passage lies behind Tyrtaeus' poem.)
73 For the same reason, that their subjects are similar, there are some close parallels between Callinus fr 1 and several passages of Tyrtaeus. There is no
   direct influence; at most it can be assumed that similar sentiments (eg 'fighting
   for country, wife, and children' or 'all mortals must die') occurred in earlier

examples of the genre known to both poets. But such subjects are appropriate to the form, and the parallels may be fortuitous.

74 'Tyrtaios über die wahre ΑΡΕΤΗ' Sitz. Berlin 23 (1932) 537–68 = Scripta Minora II 75–114 = Die griechische Elegie ed G. Pfohl, Wege der Forschung 129 (1972) 103–45; cf also Paideia I (²1935) 125ff.

75 Snell, Die Entdeckung des Geistes (⁵1980) 151ff, follows Jaeger in his general outline, but several remarks in his chapter make it apparent that he finds the new 'inner' life of the Lyric Age relevant (cf Tyrtaios und die Sprache des Epos Hypomnemata 22 [1969] passim), while Jaeger thinks that Tyrtaeus is as yet unaffected by the Ionian discovery of the individual. Fränkel (Dichtung und Philosophie 386) definitely finds much 'spiritualization' in Tyrtaeus' poems, especially fr 12, but for him this is evidence of its late date. Cf also C.M. Bowra, Early Greek Elegists (1938) 39ff.

76 If we knew that ὁ τρέσας was already a terminus technicus in Tyrtaeus' time (cf Hdt. 7.231, Plut. Ages. 30), then the change in line 14 would also be important.

77 Greek Lyric Poetry (1967) 177f

78 Cf below Ch 2 n 80.

79 I cannot follow Davison's skepticism (Eranos 53 [1955] 128ff = From Archilochus to Pindar [1968] 73ff) about 'allusions' in lyric poetry to the extent of rejecting this one.

80 Compare further Archil. frr 13.5–7; 131–2; Sol. fr 13.33–70; the many passages in the Theognidea which speak of the ignorance of men and the ability of the gods to reverse human fortunes; Sol. fr 17 and Hes. fr 303; Hes. Op. 483f; Soph. Aj. 131–3; etc. On the 'ephemeral' nature of man, see H. Fränkel, TAPA 77 (1946) 131–45 = Wege und Formen 23–39 (in German translation); M. Dickie, ICS 1 (1976) 7–14. Fränkel wants the word ἐφήμερος to mean 'variable,' 'subject to change,' and relates it to the idea that archaic man felt himself helpless in the grip of external forces; Dickie supports the meaning 'short-lived,' 'mortal.' Semonides fr 1 shows that the two are reconcilable. Human beings are mortal, he says (Dickie's interpretation); unlike the immortals, they know nothing, and are therefore victims of circumstance (Fränkel's interpetation). There is such a thing as lyric ἀμηχανία; but whether it applies to the whole of contemporary society, or signals the arrival of the 'Lyric Age,' is another matter.

81 For a different view see M. Griffith, 'Man and the Leaves: A Study of Mimnermos fr 2' CSCA 8 (1975) 73–88.

82 Sitz. Berlin (1926) 69–85 = Scripta Minora I 315–37. R. Pfeiffer, Philol. 84 (1929) 146 n 9 = Ausgewählte Schriften 50 n 9, follows Jaeger and suggests further that Solon is influenced by Hes. Op. 133ff; the parallel is very weak. See further W. Nestle, Hermes 77 (1942) 129–35 = 'Solon und die Odys-

see' in *Die griechische Elegie* ed G. Pfohl, Wege der Forschung 129 (1972) 205–13.

83 The non-theological nature of this poem is emphasized by A. Spira, 'Solons Musenelegie' in *Gnomosyne: Festschrift für Walter Marg* (1981) 177–96, esp 190f with references to earlier literature. For fr 13 see below Ch 2 p 79f. Even the *Odyssey* passage is not primarily a theodicy; its purpose is well explained by literary considerations, and its theology is belied by Poseidon's actions.

84 The winds in Solon are going in an un-Homeric direction (from the earth upwards).

85 However, insofar as the Latin poets are at least partly dependent on Sappho, who makes her trampled flower a lonely one, one cannot be too dogmatic. But Sappho is often unique.

86 *BICS* 16 (1969) 133f

87 See also the text in Page, *Sappho and Alcaeus* 303.

88 Page, ibid 306 n 2

89 See Ch 2 p 59.

90 'Sappho and Diomedes' *MphL* 1 (1975) 37–49

91 See *Il.* 22.441 and Burnett, *Three Archaic Poets* 250.

92 Cf Wilamowitz, *Sappho und Simonides* 259. Other similes in lyric illustrating this precept are: Archil. frr 41, 43; Theog. 449ff, 486, 576, 1249ff; Semon. fr 7.37f; Sapph. fr 96.7ff; Alcm. *PMG* 1.46ff, 1.54, 3.66ff; Ibyc. *PMG* 282(a) 42f, 287.6, 314; Simon. *PMG* 521.3. In metaphors: Theog. 257, 602, 847f.

93 As Dr G.O. Hutchinson suggests to me. See now R. Renehan, *Harv. Stud.* 87 (1983) 2.

94 *Dichtung und Philosophie* 150 (tr Hadas and Willis 135)

95 Cf further frr 13.10; 185.3–6; 191; 193; Hippon. fr 115 (the Strasbourg epode) 16.

96 ποη[φόρους or -τρόφους. Either would be a ἅπαξ λεγόμενον, but also an epic-like compound. The phrase is a sexual metaphor; cf 'coping-stone' and 'gates' for parts of the female anatomy in the same poem, as well as the periphrases τέρψιες θεῆς in line 13 and τὸ θεῖον χρῆμα in line 15 (meaning 'sex,' Hesych. π839 Schmidt; the entry was first noticed by E. Degani, *QUCC* 20 [1975] 229). For sexual metaphors, certain or possible, in other fragments see West, *Studies* on frr 34, 41, 67, 188–91, Hippon. fr 57; compare also Archil. fr 252, with testimonium.

97 In fr 41 (where ὥσ(τε) may belong to the poem) and fr 43, the similes (cf above p 40 and n 92) may also encourage the use of epic diction.

98 Γαστροδώρωι is a misprint in *PMG*.

99 This is probably the spirit of Archil. fr 117, since Glaucus is a friend. Fr 19.1

τοῦ πολυχρύσου Γύγεω may be counted, although the invective is not aimed directly at Gyges.

100 πλάζειν could be an ordinary word in old Ionic; and ἀκρόκομοι might be at least partially justified by adding yet another category to Harvey's list: the names of peoples encourage epithets. However, most peoples so encumbered are legendary ones (so that their epithets fall into the category of 'heroic contexts'). Historical peoples with epithets: Critias Vors. 88 β 2.11 (West, Iambi et Elegi ıı 53); Mimn. fr 14.3; Alc. fr 130b 17f; Simon. PMG 519 fr 32.1; Pind. Pyth. 1.78, Isthm. 7.10; fr 105(b) 1; also Pind. fr 192, Bacchyl. 18.2, 5.1, but these may be partly conditioned by the elevated tone of all invocations.

101 Cf further J. Griffin, Homer on Life and Death (1980) 141f.

102 'Espressioni formulari nell' elegia arcaica' QUCC 16 (1973) 7–78

103 One notes in these groups of parallels that the similarity, while it can be strictly verbal, is often a matter of structure. A study of the transformations which occur in such groups as these would be a good place to start if one were trying to clarify the role of structure in the Homeric formula. In inscriptions, the phenomenon here discussed is further exemplified by the standard language developed by the authors for various recurring contexts (eg σῆμα/μνῆμα τόδ᾽ ἐστίν ; ἀγαθοῦ καὶ σώφρονος ἀνδρός ; so-and-so μ᾽ ἀνέθηκε to such-and-such a god; περικαλλὲς ἄγαλμα ; etc).

104 In epic cf Hes. Th. 65–70, hAp. 515, hMerc. 153, 423, 455, hHom. 32.20. See also D.A. Campbell, The Golden Lyre: The Themes of the Greek Lyric Poets (1983) ch 8.

105 Wilamowitz, Hermes 32 (1897) 257 = Kleine Schriften ı 215

106 In epic: 'flower of youth' eg Il. 13.484, Hes. Th. 988 (~ hMerc. 375); πολυήρατος with ἥβη Od. 15.366, Hes. frr 30.31, 205.2, hVen. 225, 274.

107 See D.A. Campbell, Greek Lyric Poetry (1967) 162; C.M. Bowra, Early Greek Elegists (1938) 15; W.J. Verdenius, Mnemos. ser 4 25 (1972) 1–8. There are several 'elegiac formulae' in the poem; with line 7 γῆς πέρι καὶ παίδων compare Tyrt. fr 12.34, fr 10.13; for line 15 cf above p 44.

108 In line 8 he appears to break off abruptly, but then returns to the point just made that death is inescapable; the connection between lines 15 and 16 is clumsy.

109 Cf below Ch 2 p 77.

110 At fr 13.3f there is an interesting parallel with an inscription: καὶ πρὸς ἁπάντων / ἀνθρώπων αἰεὶ δόξαν ἔχειν ἀγαθήν ; IG XIV 652.2 (Lucania, VI BC; Hansen no 396) δὸς δέ ϝ᾽ ἰν ἀνθρώποις δόξαν ἔχειν ἀγαθάν.

111 208ff; cf E. Rickmann, 'In cumulandis epithetis quas leges sibi scripserint poetae Graeci maxime lyrici' (diss, Rostock 1884) 26ff.

112 Another word in the lyric vocabulary for music and festivity; cf Sappho fr 156.1, Anac. PMG 394(a), Pind. Ol. 7.11, 11.14, Pyth. 8.70, Nem. 1.4f, etc.

113 Of course, if we had more of epic and lyric, further parallels might emerge for these and many other phrases; as the evidence stands, we have no choice here but to note their uniqueness.

114 In the prayer to the Dioscuri, fr 34, there is a fairly large number of epicisms.

115 D.A. Campbell, *The Golden Lyre* 171, points out that the traditional phrase 'black ship' in line 12 of this poem both reflects the bleakness of the storm and contrasts with the light brought by the Dioscuri.

116 Burnett, *Three Archaic Poets* 187, notes the startling effect of ἑλίκωπες applied to the dead Trojans in fr 283.16.

117 Epic, it is true, often produces three adjectives, so that a clear distinction between the genres cannot perhaps be pressed. However, the adjectives in lyric tend to be more decorative; colour words are frequent among them. Furthermore, the adjectives in lyric seem often to be compound formations, although I have not checked this impression statistically. In Simon. *PMG* 543.10f the text is of course very problematic; see M.L. West in *BICS* 28 (1981) 30ff for a thorough analysis.

118 For the text of this and the next fragment see R. Führer, *Gött. Anz.* 229 (1977) 6f.

119 For a similar discussion of the epicisms and their poetic effect, see F. Sisti, 'L'ode a Policrate. Un caso di recusatio in Ibico' *QUCC* 4 (1967) 59–79, esp 70ff.

120 That the epic language developed is clear from the many new words and formulae in the *Hymns*. I drew up a partial list of phrases common to elegy and the *Hymns*, but not found in Homer, in the hope of finding a greater number in the later elegists; but the results were inconclusive, for these elegists have just as many such non-Homeric words in common with Hesiod. Cf in general A. Hoekstra, *The Sub-Epic Stage of the Formulaic Tradition. Studies in the Homeric Hymns to Apollo, to Aphrodite and to Demeter* (1969).

CHAPTER 2

1 The period is defined in the first instance not by its syntax but by the cohesiveness of its structure; in most cases, arranging the parts of a sentence logically according to the requirements of the whole involves syntactic subordination, but this is not necessarily so, since a period can consist of a single colon (1409b17). For analysis of this whole section of the *Rhetoric* see R.L. Fowler, 'Aristotle on the Period *(Rhet.* 3.9)' *CQ* ns 32 (1982) 89–99.

2 B.E. Perry, 'The Early Greek Capacity for Viewing Things Separately' *TAPA* 68 (1937) 403–27, at 405.

3 G. Zuntz, 'Earliest Attic Prose Style' *C&M* 2 (1939) 121–44 = *Opuscula Selecta* (1972) 18–37, at 19.

4 B.A. van Groningen, *La composition littéraire archaïque grecque* (1958) 99

5 W.A.A. van Otterlo, 'Untersuchungen über Begriff, Anwendung und Entstehung der griechischen Ringkomposition' *Meded. d. Nederl. Akad. v. Wetensch.* nR 7.3 (1944) 131–76; also published separately, 34f, 35f. More recently compare B. Gentili, *Poesia e pubblico nella grecia arcaica* (1984) 65: 'Il poeta arcaico non si poneva il problema dell'unità organica della composizione.'

6 The quotation of the first sentence of the *Histories* at 1409a28 is an interpolation (see my article cited above, n 1). On Herodotus see D. Müller, *Satzbau, Satzgliederung und Satzverbindung in der Prosa Herodots* (1980).

7 'Eine Stileigenheit der frühgriechischen Literatur' *Gött. Nachr.* (1924) 63–127 = *Wege und Formen* 40–96, cited hereafter in the notes to this chapter 'Fränkel'; the second page number given in brackets refers to *Wege und Formen.*

8 *Homer and the Oral Tradition* (1976) 78f. See also C.J. Rowe, '"Archaic Thought" in Hesiod' *JHS* 103 (1983) 124–35, who criticizes Fränkel's views of Hesiod and reaches similar conclusions to those advanced here.

9 G.E.R. Lloyd, *Polarity and Analogy* (1966)

10 Cf D. Fehling, *Die Wiederholungsfiguren und ihr Gebrauch bei den Griechen vor Gorgias* (1969) 300 n 3. The recent work of C.R. Hallpike, *The Foundations of Primitive Thought* (1979), tends in some respects toward an understanding similar to Lévy–Bruhl's; but see the review by R. Schweder in *American Anthropologist* 84 (1982) 354ff.

11 PColon. inv. 2021 (= *PKöln* II 59); first edition by R. Merkelbach, *ZPE* 1 (1967) 81–95. See also H. Lloyd-Jones, *GRBS* 9 (1968) 125–39; D.L. Page, *SLG* S262.

12 Cf Lloyd-Jones, *GRBS* 9(1968) 128f.

13 Cf G. Maurach, *Hermes* 96 (1968) 17f; E. Fraenkel, *Horace* (1957) 185f.

14 The priamel itself is a logical, organizational device, entailing parallelism; it has been so thoroughly investigated that I need pay it no special attention here. See F. Dornseiff, *Pindars Stil* (1921) 97–102; W. Kröhling, *Die Priamel* Greifswalder Beiträge 10 (1935); W.A.A. van Otterlo, *Mnemos.* ser 3 8 (1940) 145–76; E. Fraenkel, ed *Aeschylus: Agamemnon* (1950) II 407f; E.L. Bundy, 'Studia Pindarica' *California Publications in Classical Philology* 18 (1962) 4ff; U. Schmid, *Die Priamel der Werte im Griechischen von Homer bis Paulus* (1964); W.H. Race, *The Classical Priamel from Homer to Boethius* (1982).

15 See on Alc. frr 38a, 347, 140; Archil. frr 122, 130; Theog. 699–718, 903–30; Semon. fr 7; Sol. fr 24.7ff; Tyrt. fr 10; Xenoph. fr 1.1; compare also on Theog. 667–82, Sol. frr 13.1ff, 36.1–15, Tyrt. fr 11.1ff.

16 See below p 61 for a case in point.

17 For this reason I prefer Page's supplement ἀλλ' ἃ μὲν] in line 8 (μ]ὲν is a mistake in *SLG* and in *PKöln* II 33), to respond to δυσμένεες δέ in line 11, although μέν is not absolutely necessary to achieve the contrast.

18 The description of the sack is accomplished by means of a few representative details. It is unknown whether Deiphobus and the other Trojans perhaps mentioned in line 12 are chosen at random or for some purpose; at *Od.* 8.517–20 it is said that the hardest fighting took place around Deiphobus' house, where Odysseus and Menelaus had gone in search of Helen.

19 R.L. Fowler, 'Reconstructing the Cologne Alcaeus' *ZPE* 33 (1979) 17–28. Since composing the appendix on critical signs in that article I have been able to consult K. McNamee, 'Marginalia and Commentaries in Greek Literary Papyri' (diss, Duke University 1977), which contributes the following addenda: *PPar.* 71 (Alcm. *PMG* 1) iii 9, 20(?), diples; *PSI* XI 1191 (Hes. *Th.* 578), diples (one over a word in the line, then one beside each of two lines of commentary); *POxy.* XXVI 2442 (Pindar, mainly *Paeans*), fr 1 ii 1,2 (diples?), fr 107 ii 11 (chi), fr 29 ii 16 (chi on a scholion), fr 31.4 (obelus and chi on a scholion), fr 39.9 (?diple on a scholion). McNamee also discusses an assortment of lunate signs apparently related to the antisigma (114ff), and a collection of odd signs of uncertain classification (128ff). I had omitted the ancora (McNamee 121ff) as being of essentially uncritical nature; for the obelus periestigmenus see McNamee 110ff. Further study reveals the following addenda to both my work and McNamee's: (?)antisigma, *POxy.* XXI 2299 fr 2 (Voigt, Inc. Auct. 28 = Alc. fr 253 LP) between lines 2 and 3 (compare the use of the antisigma referred to on p 28 of the article); obelus, *POxy.* VI 854 (Archil. fr 4) 5; diples, *POxy.* XV 1788 fr nov (*POxy.* XXIII Addenda p 105 = Alc. fr 128A) 2 (?), 3. There may be a diple at *POxy.* XXI 2293 fr 1 (Sapph. fr 90a) ii 20 (a commentary); the recently published commentary *POxy.* L 3542 does contain one at col ii 3. According to the scholion on Alc. fr 117(b) 40c, there was an ἄλογος beside the verse; on this sign see Lobel *POxy.* XXI p 142.

20 *ZPE* 44 (1981) 183–4. The same objection applies to the solution proposed by D.L. Page in *Lyrica Graeca Selecta* (1968) 76, which I did not consider in the earlier discussion. See further A.M. van Erp Taalman Kip, *Mnemos.* ser 4 37 (1984) 8ff (who, however, has not seen Koenen's note).

21 Cf H. Lloyd-Jones, *GRBS* 9 (1968) 135.

22 G. Mueller, 'De Aeschyli Supplicum tempore atque indole' (diss, Halle 1908) 56ff; L. Illig, *Zur Form der pindarischen Erzählung* (1932) 55ff; W.A.A. van Otterlo, *Untersuchungen über ... Ringkomposition;* B.A. van Groningen, *La composition littéraire* 51ff.

23 Fränkel 100 (73)

24 See further D. Lohmann, *Die Komposition der Reden in der Ilias* (1970), who demonstrates the extensive use of ring-composition and other organizational devices in Homer and the far-reaching consequences of this fact. Cf also W.J. Slater, 'Pindar's Myths: Two Pragmatic Explanations' in *Arktouros: Hellenic Studies Presented to B.M.W. Knox* ed G.W. Bowersock *et al* (1979) 63–70; id, 'Lyric Narrative: Structure and Principle' *ClAnt* 2 (1983) 117–32.

25 The reference to Pittacus depends on an emendation, but it is a fairly certain one.

26 Fränkel 114f (85f); see also the evidence and arguments in his essay, 'Die Zeitauffassung in der frühgriechischen Literatur' *Wege und Formen* 1–22. Further on this topic, see H. Lloyd-Jones in *CR* ns 20 (1970) 302f, citing J. Barr, *Biblical Words for Time* (1962) and A. Momigliano, 'Time in Ancient Historiography' in *History and Theory* Beiheft 6 (1966) 1–23 = *Quarto contributo alla storia degli studi classici e del mondo antico* (1969) 13–41.

27 Cognitive psychology would be of assistance here, but I have no knowledge of the discipline. C.R. Hallpike's conclusions in his chapter on 'Time' (see above n 10) tend to support Fränkel's views so far as truly primitive societies are concerned.

28 E. Fraenkel, 'De media et nova comoedia quaestiones selectae' (diss, Göttingen 1912) 46f; J. Wackernagel, *Kleine Schriften* I 203.

29 See Fraenkel, ed *Aeschylus: Agamemnon* (1950) on 264; the λόγος or φάτις in his examples is used to support a speaker's contention; the λόγος also may be a proverb, or express a qualification ('so people say, anyway'). It is possible that Alcaeus is picking up on someone else's poem (at a symposium), and exemplifying what the poet had to say ('Yes, as people say ... '); understood in this way the poem is complete. But I doubt it; ὡς δὴ λόγος or the like would be expected.

30 Pindar . *Ol.* 4, *Pyth.* 9, *Nem.* 1, *Nem.* 10, and Bacchyl. 15 end with the myth. Cf Fränkel 114 (85); R. Führer, *Formproblem-Untersuchungen zu den Reden in der frühgriechischen Lyrik* Zetemata 44 (1967) 61.

31 Lines 14–20 are governed by the verb ἀπώμνυμεν ; there are four participles, three dependent infinitives and a brief relative clause. This is a remarkable piece of syntax for this period, the normal tendency being to break up such long dependent constructions into a series of independent statements. See Appendix.

32 Fränkel 77f (53). Cf Wilamowitz, *Sappho und Simonides* 62f.

33 G. Maurach, *Hermes* 96 (1968) 15ff; Fränkel 77 (53).

34 *Il.* 10.284ff (quoted as a sufficient parallel by A. Cameron *Harv. Theol. Rev.* 32 [1939] 3; cf H. Meyer, 'Hymnische Stilelemente in der frühgriechischen Dichtung' [diss, Köln 1933] 52), will not justify it; the relevant part of the prayer is not as long as Sappho's epiphany, and everything in it is necessary in order to specify the nature of the god's past deed. Fortunately, the major critical problem of the poem – the degree of irony and detachment in the description of the epiphany – is not directly relevant to the discussion here. For a recent study see R. Jenkyns, *Three Classical Poets: Sappho, Catullus and Juvenal* (1982) 8ff.

35 For example, Page, *Sappho and Alcaeus* 18

36 Fränkel 122 (92)

37 *Sappho and Alcaeus* 53
38 We might describe this effect as one of 'protasis and apodosis,' for when Anactoria's name is mentioned, it is instantly clear that she has been uppermost in the poet's mind from the start. G.W. Most, 'Sappho Fr. 16.6–7L-P' *CQ* ns 31 (1981) 11–17, makes some good points about the differences between rhetoric and logic in connection with a poem such as this one (although his interpretation differs substantially from mine). For complete criticism and bibliography on this controversial poem see Burnett, *Three Archaic Poets* 278ff.
39 See '"Every Time I Look at You ..."': Sappho Thirty-One' *TAPA* 110 (1980) 255–61, with complete bibliography.
40 We would not call them periods according to the criteria in the Appendix, but the second sentence clearly has been thought out in advance, since it leads up to the summation in τεθνάκην δ' ὀλίγω 'πιδεύης φαίνομ' ἐμ' αὔται.
41 A.P. Burnett, 'Desire and Memory (Sappho Frag. 94)' *CP* 74 (1979) 16–27; *Three Archaic Poets* 293ff.
42 See further below n 44.
43 See below p 70f. Note that at *PMG* 3.70, after comparing the choregos to a star, Alcman uses the verb διέβα to describe her movement in the chorus.
44 However, in both the passages cited the simple verb φοιτᾶν is actually used (though admittedly in Homer the term 'simple verb' is inappropriate), which can be translated 'wander' at *Il.* 24.533. In the *Hymn*, the addition of ἔνθα καὶ ἔνθα also helps to impart the sense of 'wandering,' as does πολλάκι with similar verbs in lines 12 and 13; πόλλα could be said with these parallels to have the same effect in our passage of Sappho.

Two other passages which might be thought to show that ζαφοίταισα by itself can mean 'wander' should be mentioned. The first is Hdt. 1.60.5: οἱ μὲν δὴ ταῦτα διαφοιτέοντες ἔλεγον, αὐτίκα δὲ ἔς τε τοὺς δήμους φάτις ἀπίκετο ὡς Ἀθηναίη Πεισίστρατον κατάγει, καὶ ⟨οἵ⟩ ἐν τῶι ἄστεϊ πειθόμενοι κτλ. The heralds do not wander far and wide in different directions, but as what precedes shows, travel along the road ahead of Peisistratus; *from there* the rumour spreads (αὐτίκα δὲ ἔς τε τοὺς δήμους ... καὶ οἱ ἐν τῶι ἄστεϊ says Herodotus, following the direction of the heralds' progress). The text should be translated, 'As they went along, they broadcast this propaganda.' Xenophon, *Cyn.* 3.3, says of hounds αἱ δὲ ὑψηλαὶ καὶ αἱ ἀσύμμετροι ἀσύντακτα ἔχουσαι τὰ σώματα βαρέως διαφοιτῶσιν. LSJ, translating 'go backwards and forwards,' adds on this passage 'of hounds on the scent.' Hounds looking for a scent go back and forth, but when they've got it they move with a purpose. Xenophon's usage may be translated as 'move along'; they 'carry themselves heavily.'
45 Cf Sapph. fr 154 πλήρης μὲν ἐφαίνετ' ἀ σελάννα / αἰ δ' ὡς περὶ βῶμον ἐστάθησαν.
46 σελάννα : Page rightly objects that μήνα is unlikely to have replaced σελάννα,

but stranger things have happened. On the meaning of βροδοδάκτυλος, it is enough that the moon should be red or surrounded by a red haze. ῥοδοδάκτυ-λος ἠώς refers only in part part to the fingers of physical light; they are also – and mainly – the fingers of ᾿Ηώς. The imaginative power of the ancients which enabled them to see the person behind the phenomenon cannot be underesti-mated. The imagination here, untroubled by reason, permits ἀ βροδοδάκτυλος σελάννα; perhaps it is assisted by some kind of loose analogy with ἠώς (ie that they are both sources of light). Note also the force of 'reaching out' in φάος δ᾿ ἐπίσχει θάλασσαν ἐπ᾿ ἀλμύραν, 9f. See further R. Renehan, *Harv. Stud.* 87 (1983) 15–20; R. Janko, *Mnemos.* ser 4 35 (1982) 322–3.

47 ᾿Αλκαίου μέλη (1927) lxxivff; cf Page, *Sappho and Alcaeus* 90. A great deal of confidence cannot be placed in these categories; see A.W. Gomme, *JHS* 77 (1957) 265–6.

48 Fr 105.6f Kassel-Austin; see Page, *Sappho and Alcaeus* 91. For further criticism of the controversial middle section of this poem see Burnett, *Three Archaic Poets* 306ff, with bibliography.

49 For orientation in the large bibliography see D.L. Page, *Alcman: The Parthen-eion* (1951, repr 1979); C. Calame, *Les choeurs de jeunes filles en Grèce archaïque* (1977), especially vol II; id ed *Alcman* (1983); M. Vetta, 'Studi recenti sul primo *Partenio* di Alcmane' *QUCC* ns 10 (1982) 127–36.

50 ἐγὼν δ᾿ ἀείδω ᾿Αγιδῶς τὸ φῶς· ὁρῶ ϝ᾿ ὧτ᾿ ἄλιον, ὅνπερ ἄμιν ᾿Αγιδὼ μαρτύρεται φαίνην. The Greek actually says '(calls to witness for us) to shine,' ie 'asks to be our witness by shining' (Wilamowitz, *Hermes* 32 [1897] 253ff = *Kleine Schriften* I 211ff), as opposed to 'asks to shine (as our witness),' as most translate; but there is perhaps not much difference between the two, and we can accept the latter translation as more comfortable En-glish. Wilamowitz complains that 'shining' in itself makes no sense; he wants φαίνην to mean 'reveal (that Agido is beautiful).' This involves taking ᾿Αγιδῶς τὸ φῶς, or just the implication of ὁρῶ ϝ᾿ ὧτ᾿ ἄλιον that Agido is beautiful, as the object of φαίνην, neither of which will do; Page calls the ellipse 'hideous' (*Alcman: The Partheneion* 85). 'Shining' for Helios is the same as 'seeing,' so 'witness by shining' makes good sense (cf West, *CQ* ns 20 [1970] 205 n 4).

51 At first glance this interpretation contradicts the evidence of lines 60ff, which must refer to some part of the ceremonies at hand, and which certainly refer to nocturnal activity, whatever their precise meaning. The dilemma can easily be resolved by supposing that the ceremony began, say, half an hour before first light, and continued until after the sun was up. The present tenses in 60ff present no difficulty if the events referred to took place a short while before, and are regarded by the chorus as one part of a larger, ongoing ceremony.

52 K. Dietel, 'Das Gleichnis in der frühen griechischen Lyrik' (diss, München 1939) 108f.

53 I need hardly point out that to read αὖτα for αὐτά is not an emendation, only an interpretation of what is transmitted. Several editors have in fact printed αὖτα, but with different interpretations from the one given here, which is essentially van Groningen's *(Mnemos.* ser 3 3 [1936] 247ff) outfitted with some new arguments. Van Groningen, however, continued to read αὐτά in 45, and we have divergent views of other parts of the poem.

54 Line 101 may refer to Agido, to balance Hagesichora in 90ff. If, however, 101 refers to Hagesichora, then I admit that she has the upper hand (although there would still be room for a last, brief reference to Agido in the closing lines, as M. Puelma, мн 34 [1977] 49, assumes).

55 Note that in lines 56ff the same pattern recurs; the summary statement of Hagesichora's beauty ( Ἀγησιχόρα μὲν αὖτα) serves also to lead into the next section.

56 On stanza and content see the references in E. Fraenkel's edition of the *Agamemnon* II 135 n 2.

57 Fränkel 80f (56f); cf *Dichtung und Philosophie* 150, 153, 168.

58 *Studies* 119, following Adrados, *pp* 11 (1956) 40; see also Burnett, *Three Archaic Poets* 73f.

59 For mock-epic in the Cologne piece see above Ch 1 p 41f. In fr 23, the phrase ἵλαον θυμὸν τίθεο, although it can be used in non-religious contexts *(Il.* 9.639), may be interpreted as a religious formula, or at least an expression of great solemnity. If 'city' in 17 is a metaphorical expression, then the language of 18ff is pompous and grandiose.

60 Cf L. Koenen, *Poetica* 6 (1974) 499.

61 Fränkel 80 (55f); cf *Dichtung und Philosophie* 158.

62 West thinks that lines 697–8 perhaps belong to this poem; but 699–700 and 717–718 form a ring which says that only wealth gives men power and ἀρετή. The theme of the fickleness of friends in 697f is not relevant.

63 Eduard Norden, *Die antike Kunstprosa* (1898, ³1915) II 816f; *Agnostos Theos* (1913) Anhang v 355ff; *Logos und Rhythmos* (1928) *passim*.

64 In Xenophanes, lines 6–9 are a slight digression, but at line 10 the poet says εἴτε καὶ ἵπποισιν, with which we must understand νίκην τις ἄροιτο from line 1 – exactly as in Theog. 702–13. On this topic of symmetry and enjambment see further below, p 77.

65 ἀνάλωσιν, 903; δαπανῶν, 913 (cf 924); οὑπιτυχών, 918; ἄκαιρα, 919; ὑπάγω φρένα τέρψας, 921; γένει, 928; perhaps θέσθαι in 924 may also be included, but cf *Od.* 13. 207 (which Meister deleted because of the unparalleled construction οὔτε … οὐδέ).

66 Exact balance in single lines: 158; 217 ~ 1073; 520; 528; 558; 831; 840; 1165. In a couplet or a pair of couplets: 69–72; 93f; 103f; 113f; 115f ~ 643f; 133f; 137f; 141f; 145f; 149f; 161–4; 181f; 205–9; 219f; 221f; 225f; 235f; 253f; 319–22; 337f; 361f; 425–9; 439f; 465f; 467f; 493f; 521f; 525f; 535f;

537f; 559f; 591–4; 613f; 627f; 647f; 655f; 797f; 809f; 845f; 857–60; 871f; 895f; 913f; 925f; 981f; 1025f; 1027f; 1053f; 1079f; 1089f; 1167f; 1219f; 1241f. Antithesis not quite balanced in terms of lines to each side: 35f; 89f; 155f; 167f; 185–8; 197–202; 211f ~ 509f; 291f; 293f; 313f; 405f; 407f; 421f; 441–4 ~ 1162a–d; 469–71; 517f; 583f; 593f; 657f; 661f; 662–4; 665f; 683f; 697f; 769–71; 793f; 833–6; 861–4; 875f; 877f; 991f; 1051f; 1061f; 1093f; 1155f; 1191f; 1203–7; 1239f.

67 105–6; 107–8; 111f; 117f; 123f; 147f; 381f; 529f; 591f; 603f; 629f; 689f; 1133f; 1193f.

68 59f; 65f; 67f; 73f; 95f (see below); 125f; 127f; 131f; 139f; 151f; 157f; 169f; 209f ~ 332a–b; 213f ~ 1071f; 217f ~ 1073f; 223f; 267f; 279f; 283f; 299f; 303f; 319f; 323f; 329f; 331f; 333f; 355f; 365f; 367f ~ 1184a–b; 425f; 427f; 473f; 477f; 523f; 527f; 539f; 547f; 555f; 571f = 1104a–b; 595f; 617f; 619f ~ 1114a–b; 621f; 633f; 637f; 641f; 645f; 659f; 685f; 693f; 753f; 811f; 837f; 939f; 963f; 971f; 1029f; 1063f; 1151f = 1238a–b; 1157f; 1165f; 1181f; 1217f; 1229f; 1261f; 1335f; 1353f. In line 95 ἑταῖρος ἀνὴρ φίλος looks corrupt; although ἑταῖρος φίλος is a regular expression, the word φίλος usually makes some kind of sense, as it does not here. τοιοῦτός τοι ἑταῖρος ἀνὴρ κακός, οὔ τι μάλ᾽ ἐσθλός would heal the sense; φίλος will have been taken from 97. (93–6 may be printed together. Bergk's objection, quoted by West, Studies 150, loses its force if we understand 96 to refer to τόσον χρόνον ὅσσον ὁρώιης in 93. It is the so-called friend's perfidy when he is face to face that rankles.) For the manner of expression involved in the emendation cf 608f κακόν ... οὐδέ τι καλόν, and such Homeric expressions as ἔοικέ τοι, οὔ τοι ἀεικές (Il. 9.70) and ἐρέω ἔπος, οὐδ᾽ ἐπικεύσω (Il. 5.816), which may be considered as variations (positive-negative rather than negative-positive) of the figure which was later called the σχῆμα κατ᾽ ἄρσιν καὶ θέσιν: see C. Rehdantz, Demosthenes' neun philippische Reden 4. Aufl. v. F. Blass, Indices 1.2.2 (1886) 8ff; E. Bruhn, Anhang to Sophokles, ed F.W. Schneidewin and A. Nauck, VIII (1899), §208 (p 118 f); H. Humbach, Münchner Studien zur Sprachwissenschaft 14 (1959) 23–33.

69 Aldus' excellent emendation ties things up. ἐπεὶ πλέον ὤφελεν εἶναι may have been the uncomprehending effort of someone to join lines 1–3 to 4–8; see Wilamowitz, Sappho und Simonides 286, and West, Studies 162 ('it is not awareness of its impermanence that makes young beauty potent').

70 For a contrasting analysis see Fränkel, Dichtung und Philosophie 231, cf 235.

71 R. Renehan, Harv. Stud. 87 (1983) 12–15, argues that the poem is complete, not by interpreting the μέν in line 117 as a μέν - solitarium but by quoting the supposed parallels of Od. 23.295–6 and Hes. Th. 1019–20, the original 'endings' of the two poems. But both passages were modified by someone in order to graft on to them what follows. Before this interpolation they did not

end with μέν (cf Hes. *Th.* 963), and only seem to if you cut with scissors at those points in the published, Alexandrian version.

72 Much has been written on this poem; the best essay is still Wilamowitz's *Sappho und Simonides* 257ff. Two recent articles have done much to clear away confusion that has arisen since then: A. Spira, 'Solons Musenelegie' in *Gnomosyne: Festschrift für Walter Marg* (1981) 177–96, and G. Maurach, 'Über den Stand der Forschung zu Solons "Musenelegie"' *Gött. Anz.* 235 (1983) 16–33. It is useful to point out that Fränkel's discussion in 'Eine Stileigenheit' was regarded as a brilliant defence of the poem's unity against the analysts, but the question now is in what terms we are to describe this unity.

73 There have been two changes of subject since ἡμεῖς; with this subject line 3 continues. The sentence is not however a period by the criterion of 'insertion' (see Appendix), because of 'τοῖς ἴκελοι.'

74 On the syntax of these lines see Appendix.

75 In line 10 μέν is probably to be read for γάρ (so West in his apparatus), to lead into the next section.

The two versions of Diodorus and Plutarch both go back to the original poem by Tyrtaeus. If we were dealing with two different poets, then lines 3–10 would represent the actual words of the oracle, pentameters included; but the oracles were delivered in hexameters (cf next note). The alternative version of the opening couplet in Diodorus is best explained as an accident which occurred at some point in the transmission of this probably much-quoted poem, perhaps very early on when it was still known only within Laconia's borders. The two lines are entirely formulaic. Alternatively, West's explanation for the variant may be adopted *(Studies* 185f).

76 So Bergk in *PLG*; cf K. Latte, *RE* 18.1 (1939) 843; West, *Studies* 184f.

77 Cf Jaeger, *Sitz. Berlin* (1932) 542f = *Scripta Minora* II 81f.

78 Jaeger 549f (= 91)

79 Alcm. *PMG* 1.64ff has seven negatives. Cf also Archil. fr 19.1–3; fr 22; fr 114.1–2; fr 122.1f; Theog. 165f; 1203ff; Semon. fr 7.16ff; 7.51f; 7.59ff; Tyrt. fr 10.11f; Alcm. *PMG* 16; Stes. *PMG* 192.

80 Fränkel, *Dichtung und Philosophie* 175 n 9 and 386 nn 6 and 8, continues to maintain the inauthenticity of the poem, putting it roughly contemporary with Xenophanes. He argues that Tyrtaeus is directing his remarks against a false theory of ἀρετή, and that such theorizing is impossible during the Messenian War, but thoroughly at home in Pindar's day. This argument is presumably based on lines 13f: ἥδ' ἀρετή, τόδ' ἄεθλον ἐν ἀνθρώποισιν ἄριστον / κάλλιστόν τε φέρειν γίνεται ἀνδρὶ νέωι. The translation of these lines is not, however, 'This is ἀρετή, this is the finest prize ...' (Fränkel, ibid 385) but 'This ἀρετή, this prize is finest ...,' ἀρετή being parallel to

ἄεθλον (cf Theog. 699, and West's comments on Hes. *Op.* 287–92). The casual use of the word in the phrase ποδῶν ἀρετή (2) would be odd, if Fränkel were right. As for the use of λόγος in line 1, which Fränkel says is modern, it stands on a par with οὔτ' ἂν μνησαίμην in the same line and may well mean actual speech (φάτις ἀνθρώπων) as opposed to 'account' in the abstract; for δόξα in line 9 cf Solon fr 13.3f. The amount of syntactic subordination (especially in 21–32, 37–44) is the usual for the period, except in 1–12, where it is the result of the figure; and we note that nearly every line has a sense-pause at the end, which is unlikely for the late archaic or early classical period. For a further defence of Fränkel's date see G. Tarditi, 'Parenesi e areté nel *corpus* tirtaico' RFIC 110 (1982) 257–76.

81 Francke's εἰ δ' οὕτως in 11 would tie the exhortation to what precedes, but it would not be in Tyrtaeus' manner either to deliver his exhortation in such a form, or to write a four-line conditional sentence (fr 12.1ff is a special case, and the apodosis comes first at any rate).

82 R. Reitzenstein, *Epigramm und Skolion* (1893) 46 n 2, finds more significance than I do in the structural patterns of Tyrt. frr 10 and 12, Sol. frr 4 and 13, and Xenoph. fr 1; I would not go so far as to call them 'conventions.'

83 See also the text in SLG S151.

84 *Aegyptus* 31 (1951) 160

85 *BICS* 16 (1969) 135

86 Cf C.G. Brown, *Phoenix* 37(1983) 6 n 31.

CHAPTER 3

1 Later notices affirming that elegy originated in laments are of little value, since they are dependent on the etymology and, where they go back to Peripatetic sources, on the view that the funeral epigram represented the ancient and original use of the metre (Reitzenstein, RE 6.1 [1907] 75ff). Inscriptions show that such epigrams were first composed in hexameters.

2 Archelaus fr 1 West can be explained in the same way. Other candidates are even less likely. The song for Kedon, ad. eleg. 6, is in no way a lament. Simonides fr 16 West is not a real epitaph, but it is not a real ἔλεγος either if the σῆμα is already erected; the poem is presumably a sympotic piece, like Anac. fr iamb. 2 = PMG 419 (on both see below p 99f.) Antimachus' *Lyde* was ostensibly a lament, which may be enough for some, but the story of Lyde is really a peg on which to hang a bag of mixed materials; for a composition with such a personal tone as this one the elegiac metre was inevitable.

3 'The Elegiacs in Euripides' *Andromache*' in *Greek Poetry and Life: Essays Presented to Gilbert Murray* (1936) 206–30; anticipated by E. Hiller *Rh. Mus.* 31 (1876) 85.

4 But cf below p 88. See also Dover in *Archiloque* 188f.

5 C.M. Bowra, *CQ* 32 (1938) 80–8 = *Problems in Greek Poetry* (1953) 93–107, finds on insufficient stylistic grounds that the epigram for the fallen of Coronea and several other pieces besides the Euripidean lament reflect this Peloponnesian tradition.

6 ἀναγραφή Cobet, γραφή codd. The inscription is probably Lycurgan (part of his religious reforms of the late 330s, cf eg *IG* II² 334 + *SEG* XVIII 13), but will reflect earlier (Periclean) practice. J.A. Davison, *JHS* 78 (1958) 40 = *From Archilochus to Pindar* (1968) 61, retaining γραφή, ventures a guess that the information in the *De musica* may come from 'some official document laying down the rules for the Panathenaic competition in αὐλωιδία, ie something like the διάταγμα ascribed to Pericles in Plut. *Pericl.* 13.11.' Part of such a document from a later period is published by O. Pearl, *ICS* 3 (1978) 132–9 (PMich. inv. 4682, II-III AD).

7 Suidas calls Olympus (sv) a poet of μέλη καὶ ἐλεγεῖα, but nothing can be based on this.

8 Cf laments in hero-cults (A.W. Pickard-Cambridge, *Dithyramb, Tragedy and Comedy* [1927] 139f; M. Alexiou, *The Ritual Lament in Greek Tradition* [1974] 61f); note also *PMG* 878. The story of a competition between Aeschylus and Simonides over the epigram for the fallen of Marathon (on which see J.L. Myres, *Antiquity* 8 [1934] 176–8) may or may not be relevant here.

9 The examples from the late archaic and early classical periods claimed by B. Gentili in *L'Epigramme grecque* Fondation Hardt 14 (1967) 48 n 4, are all very dubious: (1) *IG* XII 1.719 = Hansen no 460. A pair of clumsy trochaic dimeters catalectic are equivalent to iambics, and do not qualify as lyric in this context, whether or not you call them lekythia. (Gallavotti, it is true, dubs the first dimeter a dochmiac: *Helikon* 15–16 [1975–6] 82f; but the clumsy iambic trimeter he quotes as a parallel rather proves the contention of the present note.) (2) Hansen no 464. P. Friedländer and B. Hoffleit, *Epigrammata* (1948) no 177 l, and E. von Stern, *Philol.* 72 (1913) 547, are correct to see this verse as an imperfect hexameter. (3) *IG* XIV 665 = Friedländer-Hoffleit no 178. More trochees, apparently; but the reading is uncertain. (4) *IG* I³ 1210 (I² 975) = Hansen no 37; Friedländer-Hoffleit no 161 ('intermediate between verse and prose,' *recte*); W. Peek, *Griechische Vers-Inschriften I. Grab-Epigramme* (1955) no 58; F.H. Marshall, *JHS* 29 (1909) 153. No one will believe that an inscription which begins 'This is the tomb of Gnathon. His sister buried him ... ' and scans ---υυ-υυυ-υυ--, offers a pherecratean and a reizianum. The line is a hexameter *manqué*, of course. (5) Gentili, in *Filosofia e scienze in Magna Grecia: Atti del quinto convegno di studi sulla Magna Grecia* (1966) 278, offers a lyric scansion of Hansen no 394, but the lines seem to me prose helped out by one or two dactylic phrases. Gentili argues that

the space left at the end of line 5 had a colometric purpose, but the inference hardly seems compelling in an imperfectly written inscription. See further Hansen in *Glotta* 56 (1978) 199.

Several other inscriptions may be briefly mentioned: *SEG* III 56 (= G.Pfohl, *Greek Poems on Stones* Textus Minores 36 [1967] no 57) is 'usually held to be prose' (L.H. Jeffery, *BSA* 57 [1962] 136); Peek's suggestion (*MDAI: Athenische Abteilung* 67 [1942] 89) that the first line gives two reiziana will convince few. The Glaucus inscription is 'undoubtedly prose' (Dover in *Archiloque* 218). *IG* VII 1890 *SEG* II 251; Jeffery, *The Local Scripts of Archaic Greece* [1961] 95 [14]; Pfohl no 131) is certainly 'prose, not verse': G.M.A. Richter, *The Archaic Gravestones of Attica* (1961) 50 (75); those who call it an anapaestic dimeter (eg C.M. Clairmont, *Gravestone and Epigram* [1970] no 6, and M. Guarducci *apud* Richter 170) are scanning falsely. For further discussion, and for a lyric interpretation of these inscriptions, see B. Gentili, 'Preistoria e formazione dell' esametro' in *I poeti epici rapsodici non omerici e la tradizione orale* ed C. Brillante *et al* (1981) 75–104; against such a reading see Hansen xi. I have not seen the work of Gallavotti to which Hansen there refers, and which he reviews in *CR* 34 (1984) 286–9.

10 Wilamowitz, *Sappho und Simonides* 218ff; D.L. Page, *Further Greek Epigrams* (1981) 11. In the light of these two examples, the use of lyric metres for actual inscriptions is best understood as the innovation of virtuosi; others might copy them (*AP* 13.19, also discussed by Wilamowitz, 217f; cf also *AP* 13.26, Wilamowitz 216, although the measures there, archilocheion + iambic trimeter catalectic, belong generically at least to the ἴαμβος), but the practice is unusual. For similar Hellenistic experiments see the other poems in *AP* 13.

11 See J.A. Davison, *JHS* 78 (1958) 36ff = *From Archilochus to Pindar* (1968) 54ff.

12 On the ambiguous status of elegy and its epodic cousins see L.E. Rossi, *Arethusa* 9 (1976) 215f; further on elegy, below n 51. Epic hexameters were originally sung, then recited by rhapsodes, then sung again by citharodes.

13 See further below p 97.

14 See, however, A. Hoekstra, *Epic Verse Before Homer: Three Studies* (1981).

15 Dover, *Archiloque* 189; West, *Studies* 23.

16 See C.M. Bowra, *Primitive Song* (1962).

17 A. Fairbanks, *A Study of the Greek Paean* Cornell Studies in Classical Philology 12 (1900); L. Deubner, *Neue Jahrb.* 22 (1919) 385–406.

18 A.W. Pickard-Cambridge, *Dithyramb, Tragedy and Comedy* (1927; second, much revised edition by T.B.L. Webster, 1962)

19 A.E. Harvey, 'The Classification of Greek Lyric Poetry' *CQ* ns 5 (1955) 157–75 (hereafter 'Harvey'); see esp 163f.

20 R. Reitzenstein, *Epigramm und Skolion* (1893) 3–44; A. Severyns, 'Proclus et

la chanson de table' *Mélanges [J.] Bidez* in *Annuaire de l'institut de philol-ogie et d'histoire orientales* 2 (1934) 835–56; Harvey 162f, 174f; F. Wehrli, *Dikaiarchos, Die Schule des Aristoteles* I² (1967) 70f.

21 H. Weir Smyth, *Greek Melic Poets* (1900) (hereafter 'Smyth') xxxiiiff; H. Färber, *Die Lyrik in der Kunsttheorie der Antike* (1936) (hereafter 'Färber') *Abh.* 30f, 48f; *Texte* 29f.

22 C. Calame, *Les choeurs de jeunes filles en Grèce archaïque* Filologia e critica 20–1 (1977).

23 It is difficult to determine the point at which a τόπος ceases to be natural and becomes a convention. Comparison of human singing to that of birds is natural, but also suspiciously common (a particular favourite with Alcman: *PMG* 1.85ff, 100f; *PMG* 30, 39, 40; cf *PMG* 10(a).6; *PMG* 82, 142, 166). Sirens occur suggestively at Alcman *PMG* 1.96 and *PMG* 30, and Pindar *Partheneion* II (fr 94b) 13. Alcman compares girls to the sun at *PMG* 1.40ff, to a star at *PMG* 3.66; Sappho says that the girl who went to Lydia stands out among other women as the moon among stars (fr 96.6ff).

24 See M. Puelma, *MH* 34 (1977) 5f; J.T. Hooker, *Rh. Mus.* 122 (1979) 211–21.

25 Smyth lxix-lxxv; Färber *Abh.* 34f, 55f; *Texte* 41f; M. di Marco, 'Osservazioni sull' iporchema' *Helikon* 13–14 (1973–4) 326–48.

26 P. Maas, *Philol.* 66 (1907) 590–6 = *Kleine Schriften* 221–8; *RE* 9.1 (1914) 130–4. For the mythical Hymenaios, Linos, etc, see K.O. Müller, *Geschichte der griechischen Literatur* I⁴ (1882) 25ff.

27 P. Maas, *Philol.* 66 (1907) 590–6 = *Kleine Schriften* 221–8; R. Wünsch, *RE* 9.1 (1914) 140–83; Harvey 165ff; K. Frisk, *Griechisches etymologisches Wörterbuch* II (1970) 965; P. Chantraine, *Dictionnaire étymologique de la langue grecque* 4.1 (1977) 1156.

28 Smyth xxvii

29 ' ... wohl als Figura etymologica empfunden' (Wünsch *RE* 9.1 [1914] 141); but the expression may be simply an example of the familiar analogy with crafts (Homer's bard is a δημιουργός, *Od.* 17.383ff). For 'weaving' cf Pind. *Ol.* 6.86, fr 179; Bacchyl. 13.223 (supp). For the Indo-European ancestry of these images see R. Schmitt, *Dichtung und Dichtersprache in indogermanischer Zeit* (1967) §§600–9.

30 See E. Norden, ed *Vergil: Aeneis VI* (³1927, repr 1984) on 46.

31 Paeans and dithyrambs are hymns with particular names; hymn-form can play an important role also in hyporchemata and prosodia.

32 Many are shared with prayer-form. See E. Norden, *Agnostos Theos* (1913) 143ff; H. Meyer, 'Hymnische Stilelemente in der frühgriechischen Dichtung' (diss, Köln 1933); W. Klug, 'Untersuchungen zum Gebet in der frühgriechischen Lyrik' (diss, Heidelberg 1954), *non vidi*.

33 Quoted by Voigt at fr 308. On Menander and the genres cf F.J. Cairns, *Generic Composition in Greek and Roman Poetry* (1972). Menander's conception of generic rules is, however, vastly different from that of archaic poets, who still thought the religious reasons for hymn-form very important. For criticism of Cairn's procedures see the new edition of Menander by N.G. Wilson and D.A. Russell (1981) xxxiff; J. Griffin, 'Genre and Real Life in Latin Poetry' *JRS* 71 (1981) 39–49; and in general L.E. Rossi, 'I generi letterari e le loro leggi scritte e non scritte nelle letterature classiche' *BICS* 18 (1971) 69–94, who clearly illustrates the changing attitudes to generic 'rules' in the different periods.

34 See further Page, *Sappho and Alcaeus* 258ff on fr 349; 268ff on frr 325 and 327.

35 D. Ward, *JIES* 1 (1973) 127–44; G. Nagy, *Arethusa* 9 (1976) 194; H.D. Rankin, *Archilochus of Paros* (1977) 51ff.

36 The connection of Archilochus with the rites of Demeter and Dionysus has long been noted: Welcker, *Kleine Schriften* I (1844) 77ff. For the γεφυρισμοί at Eleusis see Kern, *RE* 7.1 (1910) 1229. Hesychius reports: γεφυρίς. πόρνη τις ἐπὶ γεφύρας, ὡς Ἡρακλέων. ἄλλοι δὲ οὐ γυναῖκα, ἀλλὰ ἄνδρα ἐκεῖ καθεζόμενον ⟨ἐπὶ⟩ τῶν ἐν Ἐλευσῖνι μυστηρίων συγκαλυπτόμενον ἐξ ὀνόματος σκώμματα λέγειν εἰς τοὺς ἐνδόξους πολίτας. For the insulting of leading citizens cf Arist. fr 558 Rose (discussed by West, *Studies* 27).

37 Wilamowitz, *Timotheos: Die Perser* (1903) 80ff; West, *CQ* ns 21 (1971) 307ff; C.O. Pavese, *Tradizioni e generi poetici della Grecia arcaica* Filologia e critica 12 (1972) 199ff.

38 *PMG* 199; ἐκ τῆς †σακατου Ἀργείου Ἰλίου Πέρσιδος, codd. The emendation Σακάδου τοῦ or Σακάδα τοῦ is Casaubon's; see Schweighäuser *ad loc.* For the conjecture Ἀγία τοῦ (C.F. Hermann, adopted by Kaibel) see Bethe, *RE* 7.2 (1912) 2205; E. Hiller *Rh. Mus.* 31 (1876) 87.

39 Simonides, according to a confused notice in the *Suda*, wrote a poem called ἡ ἐπ' Ἀρτεμισίωι ναυμαχία in elegiacs, and one called ἡ ἐν Σαλαμῖνι μελικῶς (*PMG* 532); the fragments of the first are not elegiac. Behind the notice may lie a record of a victory for μέλη τε καὶ ἐλεγεῖα μεμελοποιημένα (see above p 87f for this phrase), with the names of the compositions appended. Cf further West, *Iambi et Elegi* II 112.

40 The style of citharody and dithyrambs gradually became indistinguishable. Phrynis was first an aulete, then trained as a citharode under Aristoclides (*Suda* sv Φρῦνις). Philoxenus introduced monody into dithyrambs (ps.-Plut. *De musica* 1142a), and Timotheus introduced a chorus into citharodic nomes (Clem. Al. *Strom.* 1.78.5). Timotheus' *Scylla* (*PMG* 793–4) was sung to the aulos (Aristotle calls it a dithyramb).

41 His city is not known, but he is assumed to be from the West.

42 Emil (Aemilius) Reisch, 'De musicis Graecorum certaminibus' (diss, Vienna 1885) 7

43 Primary material for the archaic and classical periods in Hansen; there is a useful selection of Hellenistic epigrams in Page, *Epigrammata Graeca* (1975). For discussion see R. Reitzenstein, *Epigramm und Skolion* (1893); Wilamowitz, *Sappho und Simonides* 192–232; J. Geffcken, 'Studien zum griechischen Epigramm' in *Das Epigramm* ed G. Pfohl (1969) 21–46; West, *Studies* 19–21.

44 P.A. Hansen in *Glotta* 56 (1978) 199f; M.B. Wallace, 'The Metres of Early Greek Epigrams' in *Greek Poetry and Philosophy: Studies in Honour of Leonard Woodbury* ed D.E. Gerber (1984) 303–17.

45 Cf Wilamowitz, *Sappho und Simonides* 211.

46 In the Palatine Anthology the next poem reads:

βαιὰ φαγὼν καὶ βαιὰ πιὼν καὶ πολλὰ νοσήσας
ὀψὲ μὲν ἀλλ' ἔθανον· ἔρρετε πάντες ὁμοῦ.

This is a poor and confusing addition to the first couplet, and may be either a continuation composed at a later date by another hand, or a separate poem that has lost its opening couplet. In either case Timocreon's epitaph has inspired imitation. If the word-play in this poem should make anyone suspect a Hellenistic date, see R. Kassel, 'Dichterspiele' *ZPE* 42 (1981) 11ff for numerous examples of poetic exuberance from earlier times. For anaphora with πολλά see eg Stes. *PMG* 187, Anac. *PMG* 388.7–8 (also, perhaps, an example of sympotic invective).

47 'Studia Pindarica I–II' *California Publications in Classical Philology* 18 (1962) 1–92

48 For the conventions of the epinician see R. Hamilton, *Epinikion: General Form in the Odes of Pindar* (1974); M.R. Lefkowitz, *The Victory Ode* (1979); F.J. Nisetich, tr *Pindar's Victory Songs* (1980) 40–55. For general discussion of the critical problem in Pindar see David C. Young, 'Pindaric Criticism' in *Pindaros und Bakchylides* ed W.M. Calder, III and J. Stern (1970) 1–95; H. Lloyd-Jones, *JHS* 93 (1973) 109–37; id in Nisetich vii–ix; A.J. Podlecki, *The Early Greek Poets and their Times* (1984) ch 8, with references; R.L. Fowler in *Greek Poetry and Philosophy: Studies in Honour of Leonard Woodbury* ed D.E. Gerber (1984) 122–3, with references.

49 Cf in general M.R. Lefkowitz, 'ΤΩ ΚΑΙ ΕΓΩ: The First Person in Pindar' *Harv. Stud.* 67 (1963) 177–253.

50 For Tyrtaeus' poetry as derivative from Ionic, see Dover in *Archiloque* 190ff. The opposite point of view, that elegy had an independent mainland tradition stretching back into the Dark Ages, will be found in the books and articles cited above, Ch 1 n 20. One argument advanced is that the loss of many native dialectal features in Hesiod and Tyrtaeus is the result of transmission

through Athens. One may wonder, however, why this should make Tyrtaeus look Ionic; and what are we to make of the post-migration Ionic forms in Solon? Another mysterious argument is that elegiac inscriptions are written in dialect (and when they pass from the stones into the book tradition, like the epitaph for the Corinthian dead from the battle of Salamis, they are translated into Ionic). Since no dialectal inscription can be produced from before the mid-sixth century, this argument is useless for the history of the genre in the Dark Ages. (Some examples have been claimed, but see Gentili in *L'Epigramme grecque* Fondation Hardt 14 [1968] 50 n 1.) The metre and form were by 550 universally known; any sense of borrowing from another culture would have disappeared. Moreover, elegiac was a versatile metre (like the hexameter before it); it did not develop the same distinctive generic associations as, say, dactylo-epitrites.

51 Carlo Pavese, *Tradizioni e generi poetici* 199ff, believes that the type of musical accompaniment, in conjunction with the subject-matter, distinguished the genres in archaic Greece. This is his scheme:

|  | Recitative | Accompanied |
|---|---|---|
| 'Objective' poetry | Rhapsody (themes: hymns; heroic and heroic-comic poetry; didactic poetry.) | Citharody (themes: hymns; heroic poetry; erotic poetry.) |
| 'Subjective' poetry | Elegy and Iambus | 'Lyric' (melic), further sub-divided into monody and choral lyric |

There are no major distinctions in content between elegy, iambus, and melic poetry. Melic poetry is distinguished from elegy and iambus by its music and its more complicated metres, which in turn engender a higher degree of stylistic accomplishment.

There are several objections to this neat analysis. (1) It is uncertain that it corresponds in all respects to criteria which the poets themselves felt distinguished the genres. If 'subjective' refers only to the use of the first person singular pronoun, it is not especially significant as a criterion; what is important is the poet's relationship to the occasion. If he is speaking completely on behalf of the audience, then 'subjective' has the wrong associations. The division of lyric into monodic and choral has no ancient authority (Färber 16).

(2) Citharody is too firmly placed under 'objective' poetry; conversely, elegy's wide range of subjects allows some fairly 'objective' content (eg Mimnermus' *Smyrneis*). 'Heroic-comic' poetry belongs with iambus. (3) Elegy was not only a recitative genre. We know that elegiacs were sung at contests; but this may have no bearing on the manner of performance elsewhere, as D.A. Campbell (*JHS* 84 [1964] 67) argues. However, Campbell's treatment of other evidence for the singing of elegy is too skeptical. It is hard to ignore the information about Mimnermus' flute-playing, since he wrote only elegy as far as we know. (Indications to the contrary are exceedingly slight; see S. Szádeczky-Kardoss in *Miscellanea Critica* I [1964] 268–80. Οἰφόλιος in the Archilocheion is a proper name, and therefore of no use to his argument.) Solon sang his elegy in the agora (though presumably unaccompanied). On the other hand, the metrical form is ambivalent (see above n 12); it is certainly not a pure song-metre. With the falling into disfavour of singing at parties (*Ar. Nub.* 1354ff), it is probable that elegies were spoken.

One final point remains. In Chapter 1 (n 25) the issue was raised whether Archilochus had a clear sense of genre. This problem was relevant to the existence and nature of the poet's non-epic predecessors. It is true that the period in which metres chosen for the same subject-matter showed the greatest flexibility was the early archaic period (Archilochus and Solon). By the late sixth century, the elegiac metre was used much more consistently, in inscriptions as well; West suggests that 'its victory is perhaps a symptom of the Greeks' increasing sensitivity to form' (*Studies* 19). Our argument has been that metre is not the sole determining factor in the genres; this changes the nature of the question. Flexibility in metre does not mean a loose generic sense; Solon's poems are all written in the same genre. Elegy has turned out not to be a genre at all. Archilochus wrote only one such, ἴαμβοι, and if West's description of it is correct, the poet cannot have been confused about its nature.

APPENDIX

# Periodic Structures in Archaic Poetry

Although it is not directly relevant to the concerns of chapter 2, it may be useful to take the syntax of Alc. fr 129.14–20 (p 64) as the starting point for a discussion of 'periodicity' in the archaic period: the state of syntactic development. (The reason I say 'not directly relevant' is that the questions of syntactic development and of organizational ability seem to me distinct. If the syntax is fairly uncomplicated, there is no implication that speakers of the language are totally unable to organize their thoughts, since as we have been arguing there are numerous simple devices which are available for this purpose from the earliest times, and which require no advanced ability in logic to execute. It is obvious on the other hand that the ability to write Thucydidean periods implies the possession of corresponding logical and analytical skills.) What we need first are criteria by which periods can be distinguished. Subordinate clauses alone do not make a period, since they can be accumulated endlessly without considering the direction being taken. F. Zucker, 'Der Stil des Gorgias nach seiner inneren Form' *Sitz. Berlin* (1956) no 1, 3–19 = *Semantica, Rhetorica, Ethica* (1963) 85–95, applies with some success the criterion of 'Zwischenschaltung,' 'interplacement' or, more conveniently, 'insertion,' in order to determine periods in the work of Gorgias. 'Insertion' occurs when a principal clause is interrupted by a subordinate one, and picks up again after the completion of the latter. (Parembole – the insertion of a parenthetical thought, such as might be printed between dashes – does not count as periodic syntax; it is quite natural, and the parenthesis will occur as soon as the speaker thinks of it.) Insertion almost certainly guarantees some logical organization. Dr D.C. Innes refers me to the usefulness of hyperbaton as a criterion, defined as abnormal word order, wherein an essential idea is postponed from its natural place in the sentence. Hyperbaton will in some cases be the concomitant of insertion, but in other cases will detect a period that insertion cannot.

Clearly, only the most general remarks can be made here. In a proper study it seems to me that participles would have to be carefully considered: conditions under which two or more are found in a sentence; conditions governing their position in the sentence. If a participle has more than adjectival force, such that it could be substituted for by an independent clause, we would want to know if there is some organizational, subordinating purpose behind the use of the participle. For example, in lines 747–52 of Theognis, there is a single question, within which we find a series of participles and two subordinate clauses. The poet wants these six lines to be a unit (cf p 75 ad loc), which would lose its force if the ideas in 749ff were syntactically independent. At Sol. fr 36.8–15 there is an antithesis between those abroad and those at home, between those whom the poet respectively brought home (line 9) and restored to freedom (line 15); the participles which describe these two groups of people are not allowed to become indicative verbs, lest the antithesis be obscured. In Anac. PMG 388.1–9 there is no indicative verb (unless there was one in the lacuna in line 3), but a series of nominative participles modifying ὁ πονηρὸς ᾿Αρτέμων in line 5; this allows the structure of the poem (πρὶν μέν line 1, νῦν δέ line 10, cf p 84 ad loc) to remain clear. On the other hand, it is plain in many cases that a participle is simply an alternative to an indicative verb, which the poet could have used without changing his emphasis.

Preliminary study confirms our general impression that archaic literature displays little periodicity. The passage of Alcaeus with which we began, although it deserves to be noticed, is not actually a period by the criterion of either insertion or hyperbaton; the information is given in straightforward order, and the relative clause is not inserted because it is followed by a new infinitive clause. By the criterion of insertion, the following passages may count as periods: Theog. 497f; 973ff; Mimn. fr 12.5 ff (the series of modifiers in 6f, though none is in the form of a clause, may perhaps count as an example of insertion; on the other hand, the components of the whole sentence are loosely piled together); Sol. fr 36.3–7; Alcm. PMG 56 (the fragment does not read like a classic period, however; the rhythm is choppy). In Tyrt. fr 10.19f, an object which comes before the verb is separated from it by a relative clause; the author then feels it necessary to repeat this object (cf p 81 on Mimn. fr 2.1ff). Hyperbaton most often takes the form of postponement of the verb; but it is often difficult to identify true cases of postponement. Distinctions between grammar and logic have to be kept firmly in mind. Sappho fr 16.5ff is a case in point:

πάγχυ δ' εὔμαρες σύνετον πόησαι
πάντι τοῦτ', ἀ γὰρ πόλυ περσκέθοισα
κάλλος ἀνθρώπων Ἐλένα τὸν ἄνδρα
τὸν [πανάρ]ιστον

καλλίποισ' ἔβα 'ς Τροῖαν πλέοισα.

The sentence cannot be understood without ἔβα, which comes very near its end; this indicates hyperbaton, and therefore a period. However, the ideas are presented in the order of their logical priority; the main proof of Sappho's thesis is that Helen left her husband, not that she went to Troy. If she had said πάγχυ δ' εὔμαρες σύνετον πόησαι πάντι τοῦτο, ἀ γὰρ ... Ἐλένα ἔβα ἐς Τροῖαν καλλίποισα τὸν ἄνδρα τὸν πανάριστον, there would be a logical hyperbaton. Examples in the early part of the archaic period where the verb is both postponed and central to the logic of the sentence are: Sapph. fr 2.16; Archil. s478.41; Alcm. PMG 1.43–5 (?); PMG 1.60–3. Alcaeus achieves a sharp effect by postponing the verb at fr. 298.22, but it is perhaps not a case of hyperbaton, since some such verb is expected from παρθενίκαν ἔλων in line 20. Hyperbaton through postponement of the verb is more frequent in the later archaic age: there are several examples in Ibycus (PMG 282(a) 45; 286.6, 12; 287.4, 7; 288.4 (?); 310.2) and Anacreon (PMG 358.4, 8; 375.3; 408.3). On Sappho fr 31.7ff, see p 121 n 40.

# INDEXES

## INDEX OF PASSAGES

## GENERAL INDEX

# Phoenix Supplementary Volumes Series

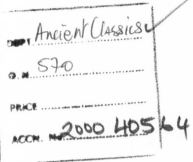